WHY WAIT?

Books by Laura B. Gallier

Choosing to Wait

Available From Destiny Image Publishers

WHY WAIT?

What Singles Need to Know About
Sex and Dating

Laura B. Gallier

DESTINY IMAGE® PUBLISHERS, INC.

P.O. Box 310, Shippensburg, PA 17257-0310

"Speaking to the Purposes of God for This Generation and for the Generations to Come."

This book and all other Destiny Image, Revival Press, MercyPlace, Fresh Bread, Destiny Image Fiction, and Treasure House books are available at Christian bookstores and distributors worldwide.

For a U.S. bookstore nearest you, call 1-800-722-6774.

For more information on foreign distributors, call 717-532-3040.

Or reach us on the Internet: www.destinyimage.com.

Previous ISBN: 978-1-60702-635-8
ISBN 10: 0-7684-3143-3
ISBN 13: 978-0-7684-3143-8

For Worldwide Distribution, Printed in the U.S.A.

1 2 3 4 5 6 7 8 9 10 11 / 13 12 11 10 09

To Colton, Madison, and Avery.

I have no greater joy than to hear that my children are walking in the truth.

—3 JOHN 1:4

Contents

Quiz

Is this book for me?

1. Do you have a pulse?

___ Yes ___ No✱

✱ *If you checked "NO," please call 911 right away!*

2. Have you ever had a crush on someone?

___Yes ___ No

3. Can you read?

___ Yes ___ No

4. Are you willing to start and finish a book about sex?

___ Yes ___ No

If you answered *yes* to all four of the questions above, this book is for you! Before you get started though, let me give you a quick heads up. There may be certain chapters you want to turn to right away; however, this book is best understood when you start in the first chapter and proceed through the rest of the chapters in the order they appear.

And with that—happy reading!

Chapter One

Isn't premarital abstinence just for nuns and nerds?

When you hear the words *premarital abstinence,*** what mental image do you conjure up? Perhaps you envision a heavyset nun sporting a stiff black and white robe, her pale, plump face bulging through one of those freakishly odd headdresses. Or maybe a certain person comes to mind—that dorky bucktoothed kid with the "I Brake for Science Fairs" bumper sticker plastered to his biology binder. He says he's waiting until he's married to have sex, but rumor has it that's just a cover-up for the fact that he has yet to muster up the courage to ask a girl out. Then again, maybe the first person you think of is someone you really admire and respect who has openly committed to abstinence.

---

*✳PREMARITAL ABSTINENCE:
One's personal commitment to refrain
from sex until marriage.

When I was young, I associated premarital abstinence with those "goody-goody" preppy types who, in my opinion, were boring, snobby, and overly sheltered by their parents. Eventually, my perspective drastically changed, but I'll get to that later. For now, what matters is what *you* believe about abstinence. You probably know where your parents stand on the issue, how your B.F.F. views the topic, and what the "in crowd" has to say about premarital sex, but this book is not about them— *it's about you, your future, and your right to choose.*

Who Are You, Anyway?

Do you remember when your mother used to dress you when you were little? In the first grade, my mom sent me to school on picture day wearing turquoise corduroy pants with a rainbow-colored knit unicorn sweater. (Yes, the unicorn's mane was made of fringe!) To top it off, she cut my hair the night before—even at six years of age I knew half-inch-length bangs that stretched from one ear all the way to the other were *not* cool.

The point is, when we are children, our parents

(or caregivers) tend to make most of our decisions for us. They not only influence our *outward* appearance, such as the way we dress and how we style our hair (God bless my mother!), but they also mold our *inward* views and thought processes. Our parents are the primary influence on our worldview,✳ which includes our spiritual, political, ethical, and moral perspectives.

✳WORLDVIEW:

How one perceives the world based on personal beliefs and what one believes to be true about God, self, humanity, and civilization.

However, as we blossom into teenagers (or in my case, awkwardly stumble through the teen years), it's time to start thinking for ourselves. Now, I am *not* saying it's time to rebel against our parents and revolt against the adult authorities in our lives. I'm simply saying that we need to begin examining the deeper issues of life and determining who we are and what we stand for.

It is equally important to come to terms with who we are *not* and what we will *not* stand for. This quest to deepen our personal sense of identity involves deciding what kind of peer group we prefer to hang around, what sort of music we want to listen to, and how we want to dress, but it is much bigger than these variables (though while we're on the topic, may I suggest staying away from unicorn sweaters with fringe manes!).

This journey is about discovering our own set of core values and developing personal convictions* that guide us through life. In order to do this, we must go beyond "*just because*" thinking—"I believe it *just because...*" *or* "I do that *just because....*"

---

*CONVICTION:
The state of being convinced, especially in terms of viewing something as morally right or wrong.

As my husband often says, *until we know what we stand for, we will fall for anything.* Case in point, young person, you've got to start looking at the more serious issues in life and making some crucial conclusions.

This process starts by distinguishing truth from lies.

Truth Versus Lies

I know, I know—you're wondering when we're gonna talk about sex. Trust me, this book is all about sex, but we have to look at some important things first—things that, believe it or not, drastically affect how you view sex.

If you think about it, humanity is plagued by an ongoing battle between truth and lies.

Approximately one-third of young women get pregnant before age 20.[2]

For example, it is the *truth* that causes a couple to take an unwanted baby into their home and shower him with the words of affirmation and love he truly deserves. On the contrary, it is a *lie* that compels an attractive young lady to starve herself to death, falsely believing she is fat despite her protruding bones.

Unfortunately, our society today is being bombarded with the bogus idea that absolute truth✶ does not exist, that we each decide what is true, and then "poof!"—it becomes true (a philosophy known as *relativism*). But how can this be?

✶ABSOLUTE TRUTH:
The notion that there are certain life truths which remain constant throughout history and apply to all of humanity.

Consider these controversial scenarios:

✶ God, a Supreme Being, either exists or does not exist.

✶ Heaven is a real place or a myth; it can't be both.

✶ The Bible is either inspired by God, and therefore perfectly true, or it is made up of humanity's opinions, and consequently, flawed by human error.

And if *you* believe one thing and *I* cling to the exact opposite view, how can we *both* be right?

Let me ask you a question. Are you just going to believe what you hear about God, the world, and yourself without giving it much thought? Are you going to make decisions about sex, love, and your life's priorities based on what Hollywood portrays in make-believe TV episodes? Are you going to allow what your peers say about you to define who you are?

Allow me to offer some advice that I really needed to hear when I was young. Don't claim to be a certain religion *just because* that's what your parents are. And don't go to church on Sundays *just because* that's what "good kids" do. Likewise, don't be an atheist *just because* your biology teacher showed you some video that claimed we all came from apes.

HAVE QUESTIONS ABOUT EVOLUTION VERSUS THE BIBLICAL ACCOUNT OF CREATION?
Log onto AnswersInGenesis.org.

And don't believe the mean things someone says about you *just because* the person who said it was popular. And for Pete's sake, don't have sex *just because* you can!

You must seek truth for yourself, and not in some half-hearted, "I will when I feel like it" kind of way. The pursuit of truth is far too important for that approach, and here's why:

We are confronted every day with truth and lies. Furthermore, there are tremendous blessings for believing and following the truth, but devastating consequences for believing and following a lie.

Go ahead—read that bold print again until it really sinks in.

The Truth About Lies

My sister-in-law, Debbie, is an ambulance driver in a small Texas town, and she recently experienced one of the most difficult days at work she's ever had. Her emergency unit received a call that a 16-year-old boy had been handling a gun that he *sincerely believed* was not loaded. He was wrong. Tragically, he accidentally shot his sister in the head and killed her.

Debbie soon realized she knew the family—she was good friends with the kids' mother! After the girl's body was removed, Debbie worked late into the night helping to clean up at the scene of the incident, which involved scrubbing the blood-soaked carpet and peeling brain matter off of the boy's bedroom walls. (Gruesome, I know.)

Case in point—*believing a lie can have devastating results*, even if one's belief is heartfelt and sincere. That gun was loaded and no amount of disbelief could change that. And so it is in life. **Our opinions don't change reality**, which is why we want to diligently seek to discover truth— *so that our opinions line up with reality!* Am I making any sense here?

Just so you know, I do believe that God exists, that Heaven is a real place, and that the Bible is inspired by God and therefore, 100 percent true, but it's not just because some preacher told me it's true. I've dedicated my life to researching the history and accuracy of the Bible, listening to skeptics' arguments, washing their philosophies against the wisdom of the Scriptures, and sincerely seeking and praying for God to reveal truth to me.

Believe it or not, my pursuit for truth not only led me to a real and meaningful relationship with Christ, but also birthed a passion in me to help young people understand God's plan for sex.

Finally, It's Time to Talk About Sex!

When it comes to truth and lies, one of the most massive tidal waves of deception engulfing this generation of young people is the idea that sex has no real significance and, therefore, needs no boundaries. These days, sex with whomever and whenever is not only accepted by our society, but often celebrated. As a result, young people are drowning under the pressure and consequences of those lies.

An estimated half of all new cases of HIV occur in people under the age of 25.[3]

Well, *I* personally believe that, but what about you? *What do you believe?*

* Is sex simply a physical act, or is there more to it?

* Does God have a plan and purpose for your sexuality?

* Is there any valid reason to wait until you're married to have sex?

Many people would respond to those questions with a big "fat" *no*, but *what's the truth of the matter? What do you really believe?*

Maybe you are not convinced that there's any real purpose in saving sex for marriage. You believe that sex is simply about experiencing physical pleasure and, if desired, making babies. Well that's okay; I understand that way of thinking because that's the way I used to believe. But eventually, my desire to get to the truth of the matter led me to... well...*the naked truth about sex and abstinence!* Now I feel I *must* share those truths with you because, believe it or not, you have a decision to make.

It Really Is *Your* Decision!

You may have parents who go out of their way to keep you out of sexual temptation—no

One in four teens claims to feel pressure to have sex.[4]

dating, no alone time with the opposite sex, and no way of sneaking out of the house at night without tripping that blasted burglar alarm! Then again, your parents may be extremely relaxed in this area. They let you pretty much go out with whomever, whenever, wherever, and don't ask a whole lot more than, "Did you spend all the cash we gave you?" Perhaps you don't even live with your parents anymore.

Either way, the decision to engage in sex or abstain is ultimately *your* decision. I often warn adults, no matter how strict their parental standards are, they can't stop their kids from having sex if their teenagers are truly determined to do so. If you're anything like I was when I lived at home, you can come up with some creative ways of getting around your parents' rules and boundaries when you really set your mind to it.

LESSONS I LEARNED THE HARD WAY!

Wearing all black does *not* make you invisible at night, and cops are highly suspicious of teenagers running through neighborhoods with backpacks full of toilet paper. Just giving you a heads up!

When sexual temptation comes—and trust me, it will—the choice to give in or say no will be up to *you*. No one can make that decision for you. You may have a great support team in your life—your parents, youth leaders, friends, stuffed animals you've confided in for years—but in the heat of the moment, *you* will decide what to do. When your beliefs about sex are put to the test, *you* will be forced to make a decision. In short, *Care Bear ain't gonna be there to bail you out!*

With this in mind, it is of the utmost importance that you have all the facts so that you can make up your mind about where you stand on the issue of premarital sex. Equally important, you must understand what it realistically takes to abstain from sex until marriage should you choose to pursue abstinence.

Sure, we'll touch on the risks of pregnancy and STDs throughout this book, but we're not going to stop there. In upcoming chapters, we will travel beyond the physical aspects of human sexuality and examine the *spiritual* implications of sex as described in the Bible. Trust me, it will be real. It will be fun. Hey, it just might be *real fun*! I only ask one thing from you at this point. Make that two things:

1. **Finish what you start.** Determine to read every chapter of this book. No matter how busy you get or what crazy circumstances life sends your way, don't put this book on the shelf until you've read it in its entirety. The subject of this

*A*pproximately 10 percent of boys and girls have sex before turning 14.[5]

book—sex—is *that* important! And don't skip to the few chapters that seem the most interesting. There's something in *every* chapter that I really want you to know.

2. **Think about what you're reading.** When I pose various questions, take time to ponder your answers. When I put forth certain challenges, take me up on them. In other words, don't just read the book to read it— get everything out of it you can, quizzes and all. That's the only way you'll see what I am desperately hoping to reveal to you.

Do You See What I See?

When I was in junior high and my social life was so lame that I had nothing better to do than walk the mall for hours with my equally penniless friends, I discovered a store that sold Magic Eye pictures. When I first took a look around I thought, *Who in the world would buy one of these? It just looks like messy spaghetti noodles slopped on a canvas!*

But as I stood there and stared at one of the pictures, something amazing happened. I suddenly saw a breathtaking 3-D image of an eagle soaring high above snowcapped mountains. I blinked a bit, and just as quickly as the beautiful artwork appeared, I lost it again and saw only the messy spaghetti.

I learned that there was a certain trick the lines play on your eyes and if you could focus just right, every seemingly ugly picture in there actually concealed a gorgeous multiple-layer image. Not everyone was patient enough to make their way around the store to try and see the hidden beauty masked on each canvas, but I loved to, simply because the images impressed me so much.

Sex can be the same way. At first glance, it looks like little more than a physical act. But if we're willing to focus on the Creator's real purpose for sex, we will see it is a much deeper and richer experience than we originally imagined. We will also come to realize that premarital abstinence is *not* just for nuns and nerds—it's for anyone who desires to plan ahead for his or her future love life.

I cannot wait to paint that picture for you! I'll start right away in the next chapter, but first, give some thought to these "Points to Ponder." Better yet, discuss these questions and answers with a friend.

Points to Ponder

1. What is your source of truth? In other words, how do you decide if something is true?

* _____

_____

_____

2. Do you think and act the way you do simply because your parents tell you to, or do you do things because you believe it's the right thing to do?

* _____

_____

_____

3. In your opinion, what is the purpose of sex? Is there anything special or sacred about it?

* _____

_____

_____

4. Should sex be reserved for marriage? Why or why not?

✳ _____

_____

_____

5. Do you like crunchy or creamy peanut butter best?

✳ _____

_____

_____

6. What do you hope to accomplish by reading this book?

✳ _____

_____

_____

Chapter Two

*What's so special and sacred
about sex, anyway?*

few months ago, my family and I went to a fellow church member's house for a get-together. I was eating a yummy taco and enjoying a friendly conversation with a man whom I didn't know very well. As we were talking at the kitchen table and getting acquainted with one another, a family pet—a fluffy dog named Harley—started sniffing one of the couch pillows a few feet away from us. We kept talking but found ourselves increasingly focused on the dog. Without any real warning (not sure what that warning would have been, actually) Harley started—well—let's just say he was attempting to mate with the pillow!

Right when I thought the situation could not get any more awkward, the man I'd been talking to, obviously just as at a loss for words as I was, turned to me and blurted out, "What's that dog doing?"

Avoiding eye contact at all costs, I replied, "Umm... he's...well, I think...he might be...uh..." And with that, I got up and went into the kitchen for more ice—not because I needed more ice in my cup, mind you, but because that was the only way I could think of to bail out of the situation. Well, it was that or pretend to choke on a piece of taco meat, but since I didn't want to attract a lot of attention to myself, I went with the "more ice" maneuver.

Instinct or Instruction?

When we witness the not-so-romantic "sniff and pursue" mating rituals of animals (I'm grateful it was just a pillow!), perhaps some may assume that sex is nothing more than a physical act necessary for reproduction. Since sexual desire is an instinct we all have, we may conclude that, like dogs, we should just indulge our physical cravings whenever we have the opportunity.

This is the basic notion Hollywood conveys—we're all just helpless victims of our sexual instincts and animalistic desires. Sex then becomes about as sacred as an experience at the grocery store self check-out register; *no need for a personal connection—just give me what I came for and I'll be on my way!*

The last time I checked, however, God is calling humankind to a higher standard than the animal kingdom. We're not to eat our babies like gerbils often do or throw poop at people who stare at us. (I personally witnessed a gorilla with an exceptional pitching arm do that very thing!)

Unlike animals, we are to make decisions based on what is loving, just, healthy, and moral, which pretty much rules out the idea of sniffing around and mating with anyone whose scent appeals to us.

So we know our standards for pursuing a sexual relationship should surpass that of dogs, but where do we go from there? How should we make up our minds about what is and isn't permissible when it comes to sex? There's only one legitimate place to turn for answers—*to the One who invented sex!*

> *"All scripture is inspired by God and is useful to teach us what is true and to make us realize what is wrong in our lives.* [It straightens us out] *and teaches us to do what is right"* (2 Timothy 3:16, NLT).

That's right, God created sex.

Think about it. Our bodies are skillfully designed to make intercourse possible. It's not a coincidence that male and female anatomies "fit together" and can create life. And if God created sex, shouldn't we seek to know what He has to say about it? Moreover, doesn't He have the right to tell us how our sexuality should and should not be used?

A Biblical Perspective of Sex

In order to understand God's intended purpose for human sexuality, we have to look at the biblical concept of *covenant.*＊ Covenant relationships are not so easy for us to comprehend these days because we are a society of contracts, licenses, and written agreements—not covenants. Unlike the partnerships and binding agreements we traditionally see today, covenants, as portrayed in the Bible,

---

＊COVENANT

(cov-e-nant):

A formal, solemn agreement between two or more persons to do or not do something specified.

---

1. Were sealed with the shedding of blood,

2. Entitled covenant partners to each other's stuff (finances, resources, support, etc.),

3. Demanded death for covenant violators; and

4. Were witnessed by God.

The concept of covenants was invented by God, not man or woman, and was created as a *sacred lifelong commitment* between parties. Believe it or not, as we take a closer look at each of these four characteristics of covenants, we will see

God's ingenious purpose and profound plan for human sexuality unfold.

1. Covenants were sealed with blood.

Historically, when two people entered into covenant, bloodshed was a crucial part of the covenant ceremony. Now don't misunderstand—no one was killed during the process! They either shed a light portion of their own blood or used the blood of dead animals.

I used to wonder, *why blood?* Why not have people cry a few tears into a jar or spit some saliva on a cloth to symbolize the sealing of the covenant terms?

After a considerable amount of thought, however, I believe it is because our blood is the symbolic representation of our lives. Sealing a covenant in blood meant a person was giving *his life* to that partnership, not just his word or signature. With current technology, we now know that our genetic identity is in our blood; thus, to shed blood in a covenant ritual was to say, "I'm giving myself fully to this commitment."

In the Bible, we not only have people entering into life-long covenant relationships with each other, but God actually initiated covenants with people as well. (Pretty cool, huh?) When God entered into covenant with Abraham and his descendants (see Genesis 17), He required that "Abe" and all of his male offspring be circumcised.* This certainly involved the shedding of blood. (I have a feeling there were some tears shed as well!)

✷CIRCUMCISION:
The cutting away and removal of
he foreskin from the penis.

And what happened when Christ ushered in a new covenant between God and humanity? He shed His blood on the cross.

Covenant relationships served a variety of purposes, but one in particular involved marriage. You see, matrimony was never intended to be some contractual agreement between a man and a woman that could simply be "voided" (i.e., through divorce) should the couple someday decide marriage wasn't appealing anymore. It was designed to be a lifelong covenant relationship! Okay, here's the point:

Marriage is a covenant commitment, and sex is the corresponding covenant sealing ritual!

Read that statement a few more times and then we'll go on to clarify what that means.

God designed sex to be the sealing act between a man and a woman who have entered into a life-long commitment of marriage. Want proof of this? Well, we've already established that in order to enter into covenant, bloodshed is required. Now think about how the female body was created. When a woman has sex for the first time, the hymen is penetrated, which causes her to lightly bleed. Keep in mind, there is no biological function or identifiable purpose for the hymen—we just know that the first time a woman has intercourse, it creates bloodshed. So you see, when a woman and a man save themselves for marriage and have sex on their wedding night, it is a covenant ritual sealing their partnership in blood! Isn't that just amazing?

Each time a couple makes love from that day on, it is a celebration and reminder of their covenant commitment.

> *"There is a way that seems right to a man, but in the end, it leads to death"* (Proverbs 14:12).

> *"As for God, His way is perfect"* (Psalm 18:30).

It's incredible to consider that children are created as a result of our covenant celebration with our mate. Think about it—life literally comes from the love and commitment we have with our spouse! (At least, according to the Bible, that is how God designed it to work.)

Now think about the tragedy of a young girl having her first sexual experience out of wedlock with an eager young man looking to "score," perhaps a backseat experience of some sort. What a waste of something profound! They have both robbed each other (and their future mates) by engaging in a covenant *ritual*—without any covenant *commitment*—with someone who is not even their covenant partner.

So, let me ask you a question: *Who is worthy to have this covenant-sealing experience with you?* That guy with the nice car? The giggly girl who sits at your lunch table? That "hottie" you've been dating for a while?

According to God's biblical plan, the *only* person who deserves to enjoy the covenant ritual with you is your future lifelong covenant partner—your spouse! Everyone else is *someone else's* future covenant partner; they have no business enacting the covenant ritual with you, nor do you have the right to participate in that experience with them.

2. Covenant partners are entitled to each other's stuff.

Covenant terms can be summed up by saying, "What's mine is yours and what's yours is mine." Historically, this took on a very literal meaning. If a person needed financial help, his covenant partner provided it. If someone went to war, his covenant partner fought right beside him. Even after a person died, his covenant partner often took care of his descendants' needs when necessary.

This is how God intends marriage to be. In my marriage, my husband and I don't look at our finances in terms of what's his versus what's mine. Our finances are just that—*our* finances. We are a blended family, but my husband does not say to me, "That's *your* daughter." She's *our* daughter. When he is going through a difficult time, it's not *his* problem; it's *our* problem. That is the covenant partner mind-set we work to maintain.

LESSONS I LEARNED THE HARD WAY!
Ladies, if, out of desperation someday, you swipe your husband's facial razor and use it to shave your legs and armpits, please beware: If you get caught, the "what's-mine-is-yours" defense doesn't go over very well!

Those are all physical examples of the oneness that covenant brings, but the Bible tells us there is a *spiritual* oneness as well. Consider this passage of Scripture, *"Do you not know that he who is joined to* [has sex with] *a harlot* [prostitute] *is one body with her? For, 'the two,' He* [God] *says, 'shall become one flesh,'"* (1 Cor. 6:16, NKJV emphasis added).

Actually, the "one flesh" existence that this Scripture is speaking of takes place in the *spirit* realm. You see, when two people partake of the covenant ritual—sex—God sees them as one. They are still two people, but they have become one unified entity and partnership through a covenant relationship. After all, *oneness is the essence of covenant.*

This spiritual oneness is made visible in parenthood. Think about it. A man and a woman have sex, and nine months later, *voila!* A life is

There are no marketed microbicides or vaccines (with the exception of hepatitis B vaccine) for the prevention of STDs.[2]

created that, genetically speaking, is half Mom and half Dad. Two lovers create one life.

The spiritual and physical connections that sex creates are a wonderful thing when we are married, but lead to all kinds of unnatural bonds when we are not, which is why the Bible warns against promiscuous sexual relationships. The "one flesh" union is meant to be shared with *one* person, unlike a prostitute, who is joined to many partners.

STDs: A Spiritual Example

I believe sexually transmitted diseases are an outward sign of a spiritual reality, something we *can* see to warn us about what we *cannot* see. Think about how STDs work. Guy A gets an STD from his sexually infected partner, girl B. Then guy A infects girl C, who then infects guy D. Even though infected girl B and guy D have never even met, he will carry her STD.

And so it is in the spirit realm. When we are sexually active before marriage, we create covenant unions that connect us in unnatural ways to people we've never even met!

Consider the following discovery:

Since covenant declares, "What's mine is yours, and what's yours is mine," what really happens when we're *spiritually* linked to a network of strangers? No wonder many sexually active singles complain of feeling depressed! Sex was designed by God to bond us intimately to *one* lifelong partner, but in premarital sexual activity, we find that we are just another soul added to a huge, oddly connected crowd of people we don't even know.

THE FIRST "MAP" OF TEEN SEXUAL BEHAVIOR
has found a chain of 288 one-to-one sexual relationships at a high school in the U.S. Midwest, meaning the teenager at the end of the chain may have had direct sexual contact with only one person, but indirect contact with 286 others[3]

Check this out:

* Sexually active girls are **three times** more likely to be depressed than are girls who are not sexually active; sexually active boys are more than **twice as likely** to be depressed as are those who are not sexually active.[4]

* Sexually active girls are nearly **three times** more likely to attempt suicide than girls who are not sexually active; sexually active boys are **eight times** more likely to attempt suicide than are boys who are not sexually active.[5]

True or false: *STDs are the result of sex.* Most people don't hesitate to say *true* to this question, but that's not entirely correct. If STDs are the result of sex, how come two virgins who get married, then remain faithful to one another, can have all the sex they want without any fear of catching or spreading an STD? In reality, it's not sex, in and of itself that causes disease. STDs are the result of ***illicit*** sex—sex outside of God's intended boundaries (one partner for life).

In summary, spiritual and physical unions should not be taken lightly, which is why sex should not be taken lightly!

3. Covenant requires death for those who forsake their commitment.

I'm glad cell phone companies and fitness centers use contracts instead of covenants; otherwise I'd be dead by now! That was a lighthearted comment, but in all seriousness, in the Old Testament, those who broke the terms of their covenant commitments faced punishment by death.

While New Testament terms no longer demand death for those who break covenant commitments, divorce *is* a death of sorts in that it destroys families and brings a great deal of heartache and destruction.

Knowing this, people did not enter into covenant lightly. They knew their very lives were at stake!

Now contrast this with our society's acceptance of sex outside of marriage. If breaking one's covenant terms was punishable by death, what must

One out of every **two** sexually active young people can expect to become infected with an STD by age 25.[6]

God think when we engage in a covenant *ritual* (sex) with no covenant *commitment* (marriage) to begin with? We are doing more than breaking the terms of covenant; we are trampling on the sacredness and necessity of covenant altogether!

Sex is supposed to be a bonding experience that uniquely connects us to our covenant partner. Furthermore, there is a direct correlation between casual sex and casual divorce. As our nation's premarital sex statistics go up, so does our divorce rate. One out of two high school youths is sexually active and one out of every two marriages ends in divorce in our country. Just a coincidence? *Hmmm...*

What happens to a post-it note that gets stuck and re-stuck to one surface after another? It loses its stickiness, at which point it no longer serves its purpose. And so it is with promiscuity. As our nation embraces the idea that sex with one partner after another is perfectly acceptable, there is no "sticking power" to sex.

4. *Covenants are witnessed by God.*

Have you ever been to a wedding? If so, you witnessed a bride and groom verbalizing their lifelong commitment to each other.

Having all eyes on us while we say our marriage vows provides us with a small sense of what is truly taking place on a much larger scale in the spirit realm. Scripture makes it clear that God Himself is a witness to our covenant commitment.

"—the Lord has been a witness between you and the wife of your youth—" (Malachi 2:14).

Earlier in First Corinthians 6:16, we read that two people who have sex become one flesh. In Matthew 19:5-6, we see that a husband and wife become one flesh: *"For this reason a man shall leave his father and mother and be joined to his wife, and the two shall become one flesh. So then, they are no longer two but one flesh. Therefore, what God has joined together, let not man separate."*

It is obvious in Scripture that sex and marriage are interconnected, and neither act is meant to be experienced without the other.

I would also like to point out that *God* joins a man and woman together, meaning He is a witness to our covenant commitment and ritual. Knowing this, it's important to realize that when we join ourselves to another person through sexual behavior (covenant actions), whether married or not, we can be sure *God is witnessing it.*

So is sex outside of marriage a sin? What is *sin* anyway? We'll answer these questions in the next chapter, but before you move on, take some time to reflect on the Points to Ponder, and see how you fair on the upcoming quiz, "Am I a good person?"

1. In your opinion, how does Hollywood (TV and the media) portray sex? As something special? Dirty? Casual? Sacred?

   *_____

   _____

   _____

2. Do you believe sex is simply a physical act or is there something more sacred to it than that? Why?

   *_____

   _____

   _____

3. Do you ever feel sorry for the "silly rabbit" in the Trix cereal commercials? Why won't those stingy kids give him a bowl of Trix?

   *_____

   _____

   _____

4. Based on the information from this chapter, describe how sex creates a covenant relationship.

✳ _____

_____

_____

_____

5. In your own words, why in the world did God create a female's body so that it sheds blood the first time she has sex?

✳ _____

_____

_____

_____

6. What does it mean to you that God is a witness when we get married? What does it mean to you that God witnesses our covenant ritual (sex) whether we are married or not?

✳ _____

_____

_____

7. Explain what the Bible is referring to when it talks about "two becoming one."

✳ _____

_____

_____

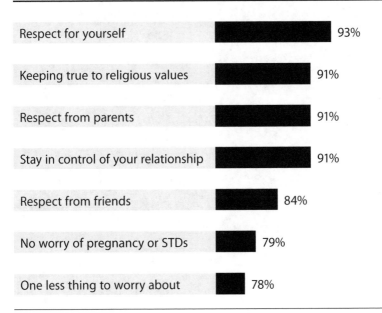

Percent of teens ages 15 to 17 who agree
with the following statements about
the benefits of waiting to have sex:

Respect for yourself	93%
Keeping true to religious values	91%
Respect from parents	91%
Stay in control of your relationship	91%
Respect from friends	84%
No worry of pregnancy or STDs	79%
One less thing to worry about	78%

Virginity and the First Time October (2003). Kaiser Family Foundation; www.kff.org/
entpartnerships/upload/Virginity-and-the-First-Time-Summary-of-Findings.pdf.

"Am I a good person?"

Put a check next to your answers.

1. Do you think you're a good person?

___ Yes ___ No

Let me guess, you checked *yes*. After all, you've never killed anyone and you try to do good things when you have the opportunity, right? I'm sure, compared to the average "Joe," you truly are an outstanding citizen.

2. Are you familiar with the Ten Commandments?

___ Yes ___ No

While we tend to compare ourselves to other people (like criminals, for example) in order to feel good about the kind of person we are, God gave us the Ten Commandments as the standard or "measuring stick" to evaluate our personal goodness. Let's look at three of the Commandments and see how you measure up.

3. Have you ever lied?

__ Yes __ No

Of course you have—we have all broken this commandment. As a matter of fact, if you said no, you're lying! And what do we call people who lie? Yep, we call them *liars* (or *no-good, rotten, "stinkin" liars* if it's someone who lied to us personally).

4. Have you ever disobeyed your parents?

__ Yes __ No

If I was a gambler, I'd bet the farm that you have deliberately disobeyed your parents on more than one occasion. (I don't own a farm, but you get the point.) I wasn't exactly a perfect angel growing up myself, so I am just as guilty of breaking this commandment as you are. Friend, you and I have been *rebellious,* haven't we?

5. Have you ever stolen anything?

__ Yes __ No

Okay, maybe you haven't robbed a bank at gunpoint, but have you ever taken something that didn't belong to you? I remember taking money out of a girl's purse in the locker room in junior high. Pathetic, I know. And what do we call people who steal? Not stealers—*thieves.*

6. Do you still think you're a good person?

__ Yes __ Heck no!

We've looked at just three of the Ten Commandments and already you and I have proven to be lying, thieving, rebellious people! To make matters worse, the Bible says God is going to judge us by those Ten Commandments. So what's the verdict on you?

7. If God judged you by His Ten Commandments, do you think you would be found innocent or guilty?

__ Umm—innocent __ Guilty

If you said innocent, I just have one thing to say— "Denial, party of one, your table is now available!" You have broken God's laws just like I have, and we are guilty. To deny that we are guilty of breaking God's laws is illogical. Our own conscience tells us we're guilty every time we do something we know is wrong, doesn't it?

8. What do you plan to do about your guilt?

__ Try to make up for it by doing good things, like going to church and giving money to the poor.

__ Hope I discover a fountain of immortality so I never have to die and stand before God to give account for my actions.

__ Nothing; there's nothing I can do about it.

If you said you plan to do good things to make up for your guilt, I have some bad news for you—God will not accept that. Think about it; would a good judge let a man guilty of murder go free because he had volunteered at a food pantry a few times? I know you've never murdered anyone, but Jesus said if we've ever hated anyone, we have committed murder in our hearts (ouch!). The truth is, there's really nothing we can do to erase our guilt. If we try to quit sinning, we will only get frustrated because we can't stop in our own strength; besides, it wouldn't change the fact that we have sinned in the past.

9. What do you think will happen if you stand before God guilty of breaking the Ten Commandments?

___ *He'll understand I meant well and let me into Heaven anyway.*

___ *I'll go to hell.*

If Heaven is a perfect place like the Bible describes, yet God is willing to simply wink at our sin and let liars, thieves, and rebellious people like us in, Heaven wouldn't be perfect for long, would it? The Bible is clear that all sinners are separated from God relationally and, therefore, upon dying, go to the place where His presence cannot be found—hell.

10. Does that concern you?

___ *Not really* ___ *YES!*

Right now, while you're young and healthy, it may be easy to say that you're not worried about where you will go when you die, but what do you think it would be like to be on your death bed, knowing you are going to face eternity and God any minute? Of course it's a terrifying thought to think that we could end up in hell, separated from God forever...and ever...and ever...and ever...okay, my brain hurts!

11. Is God a big, fat "meanie"?

___ It kinda seems that way! ___ No

If God knew good and well that you and I couldn't keep the Ten Commandments perfectly, and we would just end up in hell, why did He give us those blasted Commandments in the first place? Allow me to answer this important question. One reason God gave us the Ten Commandments is so we would realize we *can't* keep them, thus, we would recognize our need for a Savior (Jesus Christ). You see, humankind is intrinsically proud and self-reliant, but God's Commandments act as a mirror and show us how "ugly" and needy we really are. It's only when we see our true reflection in the mirror of God's law that we come to understand reality, which is that we are desperate for God's intervention and help!

12. Do you know what God did so that you don't have to be punished for your sins?

___ He told humankind we could all just make up what we think is the way to Heaven and He would honor all of our creative ideas.

___ *He sent His Son, Jesus Christ, to take the punishment we deserve.*

While there are many religions in the earth, only *one* actually deals with the issue at hand—humanity's broken relationship with God as a result of our sin. Every world religion involves earning one's right standing (righteousness) with God through good works, except one: *Christianity.* Romans 6:23 says, *"For the wages* [earned consequences] *of sin is death* [physical and eternal separation from God], *but the free gift of God is eternal life through Christ Jesus,"* (NLT, *emphasis added*). In other words, the punishment and payment for our sins is impossible for any of us to pay, so God lovingly paid it for us by sending His Son, Jesus Christ, to be punished in our place (by death on the cross). Simply put, humanity has one huge problem—sin—and God gave one mandatory solution—Jesus Christ. It really is that simple!

13. So how do I go about getting forgiven?

___ *Just say some little prayer about inviting Jesus into your heart and then you never have to think about all that spiritual stuff anymore; you're safe from hell.*

___ *Read your Bible all day, every day, and never sin again and then Jesus will accept you.*

___ *Repent for your sins, and start a new life with Jesus as your Lord and Savior.*

"Don't you see how wonderfully kind, tolerant, and

patient God is with you? Or don't you care? Can't you see how kind he has been in giving you time to turn from your sin?" (Romans 2:4 NLT).

We can't get saved by repeating some prayer that we don't really mean and then living the same old self-centered life we always have. We also can't get saved by being "good religious folk" who memorize the Bible and try to be perfect. Salvation is relational, meaning it occurs not by *what we do*, but by *whom we choose* to love and trust. We…

* ✳ **Acknowledge our sin** instead of making excuses and trying to justify our actions.

* ✳ **Repent for our sinful heart**, which means we turn away from a life of self-centeredness and self-reliance apart from God and rely on Him instead.

* ✳ **Accept Christ's sacrifice on our behalf** by acknowledging that we cannot earn salvation but must receive it based on what Christ already did for us on the cross.

* ✳ **Commit to live with Christ** as our Lord out of a heart of gratitude for the fact that He died for us.

14. Is there a formal prayer I need to pray?

___ *Yes, you must pray certain words while seated in a certain position in a certain place on a certain day of the week for a certain amount of time.*

___ *Nope!*

Just pray from your heart. The Bible says when you confess and turn from your sins and put your trust in Christ, the Holy Spirit will literally come and dwell in you and lead you for the rest of your life to the degree that you yield to His leadership. How cool is that?

15. Then will I be allowed into Heaven when I die?

___ *Maybe; maybe not.*

___ *Yes!*

If Christ is our Lord and Savior, we are welcome into Heaven, into God's awesome presence when we die, because God no longer sees us as sinners. He sees us as His beloved children! Our past sins are forgiven and any sins that we commit in the future are covered under the blood of Jesus.

So why don't we just keep on sinning? Well that's just it—once we're saved, we don't like to sin. Sure, sin is still tempting, but the Holy Spirit gives us a strong desire to resist sin and live for God. In those times of weakness when we *do* give in to sin, we feel horrible—not because we fear God is going to reject us or give up on us (remember, we're God's children now!), but because we love our heavenly Father and want to please Him.

So what do you think? Do you need to set this book down and have a little "heart-to-heart" with God? I tell you what, having that talk with God was the best thing I ever did—not because life has been easy since then, but because I now know what I'm living for.

Chapter Three

Why is premarital sex sometimes referred to as a sin?

*D*o you like brownies? How about hot fudgy brownies? When I get a whiff of those chocolaty delights baking in the oven, I forget all about my Weight Watchers diet; I'm too busy *waiting* and *watching* for the timer to go off!

For me, it's next to *impossible* to resist eating a brownie. How hard do you think it would be for me to pass up a brownie, however, if I knew for a fact that one-fourth cup of dog poo was added to the batter? Once cooked, the brownies still looked delicious and even smelled scrumptious, but the reality was each bite contained some "recycled Kibbles 'N Bits," if you know what I mean.

As you probably guessed, if that were the case, it wouldn't be very hard for me to resist eating a brownie. As a matter of fact, you couldn't pay me enough to eat a poo-poo brownie! Yuck!

So why is it so hard to resist a fresh brownie, and yet so easy to turn away from a polluted one? **Because we can't enjoy something once we know it's contaminated.**

For this reason, we are going to take a look at how sex can become contaminated. As we come to understand *why* certain sexual behaviors are polluted (sinful), we will have a much easier time resisting and refraining from them.

Keep in mind, knowing that something is sinful is one thing; knowing *why* is another.

What Is Sin?

I have good news—*sex is not a sin!* It only becomes sinful when we disregard God's boundaries for sex and lose sight of the sacredness of sex. As we look at God's boundaries, we must first come to terms with what "sin" really is.

Do you know there's a difference between *sins* and *sin?* We can all think of examples of *sins* (plural)—lying, stealing, murdering, cheating—you get the point. But what about *sin* (singular)? In the Bible, *sin* refers to the nature inside of us all that wants to commit *sins.* Furthermore, this *sin nature* can be summarized in one word—**self-centeredness**. Add your own examples of *sins* to the few I previously mentioned and you will see that all of them, without fail, are rooted in self-centeredness. Self-centeredness grieves

God because it is totally contrary to His loving, giving nature.

When we talk about sex before marriage being a sin, it helps to understand that it is a self-centered act, a concept we can easily comprehend. From there, we must know the difference between *love* and *lust*.

Love Versus Lust

Consider the following contrasting attributes:

LOVE	LUST
Desires to satisfy another at the expense of self.	Desires to satisfy self at the expense of another.
Is easily satisfied.	Is never satisfied.
Has nothing to hide.	Often operates in secret.
Brings peace.	Brings guilt.
Is open and honest.	Manipulates and disguises intentions.
Is concerned for another's wellbeing.	Is consumed with selfish desires.
Remains faithful during tough times.	Abandons when needs are not met.
Sees all that is beautiful about a person.	Has eyes fixed strictly on outward beauty.
Is patient.	Is impatient.

When it comes to sex, a person is either operating in *love* or *lust*. We can't operate in both at the same time because they are opposites (like north and south). God's plan for sex is based on *love*, not lust. Why is premarital sex sinful? In a single sentence, *because it is the result of lust*, which we know is rooted in self-centeredness and is therefore sinful.

Sex is a covenant celebration reserved for our covenant partner. To have sex with someone who is not our mate is to take something that does not belong to us. It is to put our immediate physical desires above another's long-term spiritual blessings (and ours as well). We also shortchange our future mate, who is the only person deserving of the gift of our physical intimacy.

> *Love is patient and kind. Love is not jealous or boastful or proud or rude.* [Love] *does not demand its own way.* [Love] *is not irritable, and it keeps no record of being wronged.* [It is never glad about injustice] *but rejoices whenever the truth wins out. Love never gives up, never loses faith, is always hopeful, and endures through every circumstance* (1 Corinthians 13:4-7 NLT).

The truth is, sex before marriage often involves manipulation, secrecy (hiding from parents), infatuation with outward appearances, and impatience—all of which are indicative of lust.

An Eye-Opening Exercise

Go grab a piece of paper and a pen. At the top of your paper, write "Benefits of having sex before marriage." Next, list every benefit of premarital sex that you can think of. Go ahead, put the book down and make your list. I'll be here when you get back.

Did you make your list? What did you write down? While doing this exercise, one of the only benefits of having sex before marriage that young people tend to come up with is that a person can have sex without waiting. In other words, we don't have to be patient. Now take a look at the "love" passage from First Corinthians on the previous page. Notice how it starts? *Love is patient.* If the primary reason people have premarital sex is because they can't be patient, they are not operating in love. They are actually operating in lust, which is self-centered, which is—you guessed it—*sinful.*

The Love Test—Will He Wait?

A dear friend of mine has some wise advice to share with young people, so I included it in this book (she prefers to be anonymous). Her comments

Two-thirds of U.S. teenagers who have had sexual relations wish they had waited longer.[2]

are directed at young ladies, but the same principles certainly apply to young men. Keep in mind, when she uses the word "courtship," she's referring to the time leading up to marriage where a couple is bonding and preparing for a lifetime together:

MANY STDS DO NOT EXHIBIT NOTICEABLE SYMPTOMS, at least at first, but they can lead to pregnancy complications, miscarriage, infertility in women, and, in the case of the human papilloma virus (HPV), cervical cancer.[3]

While dating, we may consider it a sign of love that our boyfriend wants to have sex with us or go too far. He thinks we're beautiful, sexy, and wonderful. But after marriage, his constant desire for sex can become a painful source of aggravation. The emotions that were so charming and amorous during courtship seem to get between the love we want to feel and the fact that men crave sex so intensely. It might be flattering at first, but what about the nights we would rather go to sleep? We have had a bad day and feel cranky, and suddenly find ourselves yelling, "It's always been about sex with you, hasn't it?" We wonder, "Would he love me if I didn't have sex with him?"

If this question isn't answered before marriage, it is so hard after marriage to believe our husband

Every day, 8,000 teenagers become infected by an STD.[4]

sincerely loves us for who we are on the inside, for more than our physical "usefulness." Don't we all want to know deep in our hearts in a way that gives real security that we are loved for who we really are?

Our husband is meant to be our protector from the world, but if in courtship, he takes a part of us sexually, with no regard to the cost, our trust is already violated. We're left thinking, "He said he'd do anything for me; obviously the exception was controlling himself sexually." Wait a minute! There are many scenarios in life where we really want our husband to take the responsibility to control himself. Do you want him to take out the trash without glaring at you or complaining? Watch the kids so you can shop for groceries in peace for an hour? Resist a seductive co-worker?

Courtship is meant to be a time of laying the foundation of trust, which is facilitated by a man choosing to honor the woman he loves, putting her worth above his own desires. Abstaining from sex before marriage goes a long way toward settling the issue that we are truly loved by a man, as opposed to merely lusted after. If he has the love of Christ, he will have constraint ("The love of Christ constrains us," (2 Cor. 5:14 KJV)).

Approximately two-thirds of teens ages 15 to 19 agree with the following statement: "It is all right for unmarried 18-year-olds to have sexual intercourse if they have strong affection for each other."[5]

Sexual Boundaries

A river is a beautiful flowing body of water, ideal for recreation and relaxation. But what happens when a river rages beyond the boundaries of its banks? It becomes a destructive flood, damaging and destroying everything in its path! And so it is with sex. Within the boundaries of marriage, it is harmless, healthy, and enjoyable, but outside of marriage, it becomes a destructive act.

> *Marriage should be honored by all, and the marriage bed kept pure, for God will judge the adulterer and all the sexually immoral* (Hebrews 13:4).

If we consider all the potential consequences of premarital sex, the beauty of God's boundary of marriage becomes obvious.

God sets boundaries for the same reason loving parents have rules—for the protection and well-being of His children. My four-year-old daughter called me "the worst mommy ever" the other day because I wouldn't let her have another cookie. She was fighting off a cold and I didn't want her immune system compromised by eating too many sweets. I wanted her to recover and be healthy. Since I had the nerve to stand between her and her desire, I became the enemy.

Sometimes we're guilty of making God out to be the one standing between us and the pleasure we feel we deserve. Young people, in particular, tend to erroneously envision

God peering down from Heaven with a lightning bolt aimed at their heads, just waiting to release it the minute they start having fun. How untrue that is! On the contrary, *all God is ultimately trying to do is get good things **to** us and keep bad stuff **away** from us!*

When God says sex is reserved for marriage, it's because He's trying to protect us, not prevent us from experiencing pleasure.

Just think about this. If all of the world's children today waited until they were married to have sex and then stayed faithful to their spouses for life, STDs would be eradicated in a single generation! STDs are a curse that operates in the earth because humankind is not doing things God's way. It's not that God is busy putting STDs on people; we invite such ailments into our lives when we push past the protective barriers He has wisely established.

Darkness results when no light is present, and such is the spiritual condition of our planet. Disease and human suffering are curses that operate in the earth because mankind, as a whole, has rejected God and His light (His Son, Jesus Christ). And how dark sexual acts can become when God's purposes are rejected! Tragedies like rape, incest, molestation, and prostitution are all the end result of using the God-given gift of sex in ways He never designed it for. Even though we tend to think of

93 percent of teenagers believe that teens should be given a strong message from society to abstain from sex.[6]

fornication* as less offensive than those acts, it is equally outside the purpose of God's plan. Furthermore, to engage in fornication is to reject God's instructions. (There's an ugly name for this—it's called *rebellion!*)

---

*FORNICATION:
Engaging in sex outside of marriage.

Sexual Immorality, a Unique Sin

First Corinthians 6:18-20 (NIV) says,

Flee from sexual immorality. All other sins a man commits are outside his body, but he who sins sexually sins against his own body. Do you not know that your body is a temple of the Holy Spirit, who is in you, whom you have received from God? You are not your own; you were bought at a price. Therefore honor God with your body.

I used to wonder what that passage meant when it said sexual immorality is a sin against our own bodies. After prayer and consideration, I now feel I have an idea what it means. Sin often involves an instrument of sin. For example, for a drug dealer,

When used correctly, condoms are highly effective against the spread of HIV. Condoms are minimally effective, however, against the spread of herpes, syphilis, Chancroid, and HPV.[7]

it's drugs. For a materialistic woman, it's money. For a murderer, it's a weapon. But when we engage in fornication, our *bodies* become the instrument of sin. The reason this is so offensive is because the Holy Spirit dwells in us (in those who are born again; see the Quiz on page 45 if you aren't sure what it means to be born again).

> *Do not let sin control the way you live; do not give in to sinful desires. Do not let any part of your body become an instrument of evil to serve sin. Instead, give yourselves completely to God* (Romans 6:12-13 NLT).

Trashing the Temple

What would you think if I told you a gang of young men broke into a neighborhood donut shop and vandalized it? They painted the walls, broke chairs, shattered glass, and ruined the place. That would be pretty bad, right?

Now what would you think if I told you that a gang of young men vandalized a local *church*. They broke into the sanctuary, ripped up the pews, painted obscene pictures on the pulpit, tore pages out of Bibles, and totally trashed the place. Somehow that seems even worse than vandalizing the donut shop, doesn't it?

Case in point—the presence of God does not live in buildings, not even in church sanctuaries. He lives in us! We are the Church! So you see, to enter into sexual sin with our bodies is to "trash the temple," and that is a wicked act.

A Politically Incorrect Word

If there is one word people don't like to hear, it's *sin*. Nonetheless, young people, we can't be afraid to use that word. Fornication is sinful, and that's the truth of the matter. And while born-again Christians need not fear hell since we are assured an eternity in Heaven based on Christ's sacrifice, we acknowledge His Lordship in our lives by heeding His commandments. In other words, ***while we in no way earn salvation through a sexually pure lifestyle, our obedience in that area is evidence that we have, in fact, bowed our knee to Christ's Lordship, which is a prerequisite for salvation.*** (That's another one of those key statements that you might want to read repeatedly until it really sinks in.)

> —*through the fear of the Lord, a man avoids evil* (Proverbs 16:6).

Proverbs 1:7 tells us, *"The fear of the Lord is the beginning of wisdom."* What about you—do you fear the Lord? That doesn't mean we shrink away from God in intimidation. It means we respect and revere God and His commandments.

We know we fear God if we love what God loves and reject what God rejects. If you're not sure what God loves and what He rejects, that just means you need to get to know

Him better. He gave us the Bible and Jesus Christ's living example so we could understand His nature.

To fear God is not to be afraid to approach Him, but rather, to fear living life apart from Him.

There are certain things about this world and humanity that God adores and other things He abhors (is repulsed by). To indulge ourselves in something God despises or disregard something God highly esteems indicates that we lack a healthy fear of God. It's as if we are saying to God, "I am a better judge of right and wrong than you are!" I don't think I'll be shouting that in God's face any time soon… okay, not ever!

The True Purpose of Grace

> *"My* [God's] *grace is sufficient for you, for my power is made perfect in* [your] *weakness"* (2 Corinthians 12:9).

We need a proper understanding of grace and its purpose in our lives. There's a message circulating in the Church today that falsely assures people sin is no longer an issue since we live under the dispensation of grace (the time after Christ's death). Many professing Christians live as if there is currently no moral law. "That was in the Old Testament," they say in a drunken state with a beer in one hand and a pornographic magazine in the other. It's true that we are no longer under the Old Testament Law in terms of the rituals and regulations, but God's moral standards haven't changed a bit. Remember, Jesus said He came to *fulfill* the Law, not *destroy* it.

I will attempt to correctly describe grace in a single sentence: **Grace does not make sin less sinful; it makes overcoming sin possible.** Yep, you can read it again.

Jesus speaking:

> *Don't misunderstand why I have come. I did not come to abolish the law of Moses or the writings of the prophets. No, I came to* fulfill them (Matthew 5:17 NLT).

You and I do not have the ability to quit sinning by shear will power or self-reliance. However, when we lean on the leadership of the Holy Spirit (God's grace at work in our lives), we can get victory over old habits, addictions, and destructive patterns that have (as my husband would say) "eaten our lunch and popped our sack" for years. This not only pleases God, but greatly benefits us! So you see, grace does not mean God no longer takes offense to sins, like fornication for example; it means we have access to the spiritual strength we need to resist and overcome temptation.

Speaking of temptation, you need to know that it is *not* a sin to be tempted. Sin occurs when we *yield* to temptation. If we don't understand this, we will be too ashamed to call on God when, in reality, we need Him the most! Should we find ourselves under strong sexual temptation, we don't need to run away from God, but on the contrary, aggressively run *to* Him for help.

How do we get God's help? *Ask and obey*. Admit we need His intervention and then obey what He leads us to do. The Bible promises God will always make a way of escape from temptation (see 1 Cor. 10:13). The problem is we don't always walk through the door of escape He provides.

If you were on a diet, which would be the best place to go study; the library or an ice cream parlor? We understand that it's foolish to sit in an ice cream shop while trying to avoid eating sweets.

TRUE OR FALSE:

"Masturbating is a great way to sexually satisfy ourselves while we remain abstinent."

Keep reading! We'll discuss this in an upcoming chapter.

So, if you've decided not to have sex with your boyfriend or girlfriend, which is the best place for the two of you to hang out together: a mall full of people or your house while your parents are gone? Obviously, it is *not* wise to intentionally subject ourselves to tempting situations and then complain that the temptation is too strong to resist. The way of escape requires using good judgment and avoiding tempting situations altogether when possible.

Goodness, this chapter is getting long! Let's end here for now and pick up again with Chapter Four's question, "What's the big deal about losing your virginity?" In the meantime, why not ponder the Points to Ponder?

Points to Ponder

1. How would you define the word *sin*?

✳ _____

_____

_____

2. In your opinion, what's the difference between loving and lusting after a member of
the opposite sex?

✳ _____

_____

_____

3. What are some benefits of having sex before
marriage? What are some benefits of waiting
until you're married to have sex?

✳ _____

_____

_____

_____

4. How much would someone have to pay you to put your socks on *over* your tennis shoes and walk around the mall like that for two hours?

✳ _____

_____

_____

_____

5. Why do you think God commands His people to keep certain boundaries (e.g., no sex outside of marriage)?

✳ _____

_____

_____

_____

6. In your own words, what does it mean to fear God?

✳ _____

_____

_____

_____

7. Do you think it's a sin to be tempted to do something you know you shouldn't? Why or why not?

*_____

_____

_____

_____

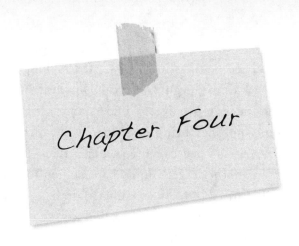

Chapter Four

What's the big deal about losing your virginity?

I have a friend who has a husband who has a brother who has a daughter who is really in over her head! This attractive young lady started having sex in high school—and didn't stop. She sleeps with one guy after another and admits to having sex with six different guys just last month. Get this—she says these guys she's going to bed with are her *friends*. How totally odd. ("Hey buddy, you wanna come over, play Wii, experience the most physically intimate act two people can engage in, and order some pizza? I guess we could go see a movie instead.")

This girl, whom we'll call Jessica, is quite popular among her peer group and is really enjoying all of the attention she's been getting since she started making herself "available" to the guys. It breaks my heart to think that she is too naive to understand what's really going on. She's being passed from one "friend" to the next so they can use her and then hand her off to another eager young man looking to temporarily satisfy himself sexually. In reality, she's not popular; *she's prey.* And those guys don't really *like* her; they just *lust* her.

Jessica really needs to understand the Coke-can principle!

The Coke-Can Principle

Tim comes inside after playing basketball with his friends and heads straight for the fridge. He swings open the door, takes a deep breath as the frosty air swarms around his sweaty face, and then grabs an ice cold can of Coke off the shelf. His desert-dry mouth begins to salivate as he pops the tab and pulls the can to his parched lips. What a refreshing sip! What a liberating burp!

Along comes James. "Hey Tim, give me a sip!" James takes a few gulps and then passes the Coke to William. William takes one large sip and then hands the can off to Peter. The Coke is half empty so Peter takes a small sip before passing it to Dillon. Dillon takes a few swigs but doesn't like the idea of drinking the last few sips. The Coke is now lukewarm and full of backwash. Dillon walks up to Tim, who took the Coke out of the fridge in the first place, and asks, "You want your Coke back Tim?"

"No way, dude! Not after everyone took a turn drinking out of it! I'll just get a new one out of the fridge."

Do you see why Jessica needs to understand the Coke-can principle? *Hint*: Jessica *is* the Coke can!

Typical guys have an unspoken rule; *sleep with the easy girls; marry the virgin.* In other words, when guys are young and eager to play the field, they tend to ignore the "virginal" girls and flock to the females who are willing to have sex. However, when they mature and desire to find a wife and settle down, their attention turns from the "wild child" who has been passed around; instead, they seek a more modest woman to marry and be the mother of their children. It's not right, but it's the truth.

Ultra-Important Point About Virginity!

Virginity is more than a sexual issue. You see, the essence of virginity is *monogamy*—not just one partner for a season at a time, but one partner for *all* time. Furthermore, virginity is more than a physical state; it is a mind-set. To have a virgin state of mind is to live with the belief that there is *one* person for you, and you are waiting for that special one.

We all know there is probably a myriad of attractive members of the opposite sex whose personalities would blend well with your preferences someday when you are ready for marriage, but there is only *one* whom God has picked to be your mate. Don't believe me? Take a look at Psalm 37:23. Surely, if God cares about every detail of our lives and has promised to order our steps and direct our paths (see Prov. 3:6), He has a mate in mind for you! After all, whom we choose to marry affects nearly every aspect of our lives. Once we are joined in matrimony, we are integrated into one partnership "as long as we both shall live." That being said, God cannot plan your future without planning who your future mate should be.

> *The Lord directs the steps of the godly. He delights in every detail of their lives* (Psalm 37:23 NLT).

Now that doesn't mean that you *have* to marry the one God has in mind for you. We have free will and can pursue a relationship with whomever we choose. But following our own plan at the expense of seeking God's will for our lives always ends in disappointment, if not devastation. It is true that by His loving grace God can pick up the pieces of our poor decisions once we acknowledge we've missed the mark, and He can even cause good to come from a less than ideal predicament. However, it's usually a difficult journey to "right the wrong," and we are not exempt from the consequences our wayward actions have caused. When it comes to something as significant as marriage, it is wise to seek God's

Plan A for our lives (more about how to find the right mate in Chapter 9).

"WHAT IF IT'S NOT GOD'S WILL
that I get married someday?" Log onto
LauraGallier.com for answers to this question and more.

God: An Out-of-Touch Old Man or a Hopeless Romantic?

Young people tend to envision God as an elderly man with a long white beard sitting hunched over on a tacky gold throne floating around somewhere in outer space. We wonder how a being living in a heavenly realm can possibly identify with the butterflies and goosebumps that accompany human attraction. We can't imagine that God knows what it's like to feel "turned on" by the opposite sex or that He understands how the human heart races during a passionate kiss. The ironic thing is that God alone created sex, along with the fantastic physical reactions human sexuality brings.

It's important to realize that God knows *exactly* what it's like to be a human, not just because He created us and is all-knowing, but because He lived as a human in the person of Jesus Christ. Wrapping our minds around the Trinity (God existing simultaneously yet distinctly as the Father, the Son, and the Holy Spirit) is enough to give anyone a brain freeze, but we know by Jesus' own testimony that He was more than a man—*He was God living as a man.* That being said, Jesus must have experienced physical attraction during the 33 years He spent on earth. We know He was tempted sexually because the Bible says He was tempted in every way a person can be, and yet did not give in to temptation (see Heb. 4:15).

> *For we do not have a high priest who is unable to sympathize with our weaknesses, but we have one who has been tempted in every way, just as we are—yet was without sin* (Hebrews 4:15).

The Bible shows us how in-touch God is with the intensity of human experiences, including our sexuality. While those who have never read the Bible may assume it's a conservative book full of child-friendly stories, nothing could be further from the truth. Sure, there are stories suitable for children, but the Bible is also packed full of detailed accounts of bloody battles, wicked villains, heroic warriors, and explicit sexual experiences. There's an entire book of the Bible, Song of Solomon, written in symbolism so that the adult content and blatant sexuality is cloaked in modesty. If you think that book is all about fruits and gardening, you might want to read it more

It seems that the reported rate of condom failure...is significant. While 95 percent effectiveness of a contraceptive method sounds good, it actually leaves a woman with a chance of pregnancy which may be considered unacceptable.[1]

carefully! It's a detailed account of passionate lovemaking and the wonder of human attraction. It also helps us understand the intensity with which God pursues and draws us to Him.

We need to know that God is romantic in nature and that He understands our sexual longings. Furthermore, His call to premarital virginity is all about romance!

Which sounds more appealing?

* Two people "trying out" one person after another physically and emotionally until they finally find the one they think is the best

* Two people saving their hearts and bodies for that one person who is to be their partner for life

God is writing a brilliant love story for you, and if you will trust in His ability to provide the right mate at the right time, He will! God has something special in store for your love life, something worth waiting for. We need to be encouraged about this on a regular basis because the hope of one partner for one lifetime is constantly being challenged by worldly influences.

The Purpose of Sex

Over the years, I've encouraged my kids to do everything with a purpose in mind. Whether that purpose is for spiritual edification, preparation for the future, or just to have a great time with friends, I want my kids to make their decisions based on more than sheer emotion or peer pressure.

When it comes to sexual activity, the purpose is to produce a unique bond between two covenant partners. The resulting bond can be as tangible as creating a child together or as abstract as lingering feelings of attachment that resonate in our souls.

"SEX AND COMMITMENT MAY BE INTERTWINED BY NATURE. Human physiological responses affect neurological patterns... As one scientist explains, those who engage in casual sex can trigger the brain system for attachment (as well as for romantic love), leading to complex, unanticipated emotional entanglement with psychologically and socially unsuitable mating partners."[3]

Did you know that certain chemical reactions take place in our brains during sex that actually cause a sort of *imprinting* to occur, meaning that the images of our sexual experiences are stored in our minds with heightened detail and permanence? Just like certain animals have chemically induced imprinting at birth so that they bond intensely with their mothers, the vivid memories and emotions associated with having sex are not easily forgotten. This is by God's design, but can be a source of torment if we disregard His boundaries for sex. Teenagers intend to move on quickly once their girlfriend or boyfriend breaks up with them, but if they had sex with that person, the lingering mental images will remain as an ongoing reminder of the intimacy they once shared. When their former lover is embracing a new "honey" at the lunch table, the emotional pain and sense of loss can be overwhelming.

The Connection Between Premarital Sex and Divorce

Each time a young person survives the hurt and devastation of breaking up with someone they've had sex with, they become more preconditioned for divorce. As previously mentioned, our country's premarital sex statistics and divorce statistics mirror one another (one out of every two teenagers is sexually active and one out of every two marriages ends in divorce). Tragically, the bonding power of sex is diminished as young people grow familiar with the pain of breaking up with a lover. They become so accustomed to the grieving process that follows parting ways with someone they have had sex with that, upon marriage, the idea of breaking up is not foreign to them.

Realizing the Value of Virginity Before It's Too Late

Even though I was a young girl at the time, I still remember my mother reaching into her

The vast majority of teen mothers are not married, but few give up children for adoption or care by others. For this reason, the mothers often must drop out of school and cannot hold full-time employment.[4]

dresser drawer and pulling out a small shiny silver box. I knew the contents had to be valuable because she kept it hidden in an unsuspecting place away from the rest of her jewelry. Upon removing the lid, my mother showed me her high school class ring. It was beautiful, but more importantly, the ring was highly sentimental to her.

Sometime later when I was a freshman in high school, I decided I was going to get that ring out of my mom's dresser and wear it to school. I thought it would be "cool." I knew it wasn't right to sneak behind my mother's back and wear her jewelry, but I convinced myself that it didn't matter since I'd have the ring right back in the box after school.

I managed to keep the ring on most of the day, but during my last class period, a girl started admiring the piece of jewelry and asked to wear it. I knew her fairly well so I felt comfortable letting her put it on. Unfortunately I was on my way home from school before I remembered loaning the ring to her! I didn't get too panicked, however, because I figured the girl would just bring it to me the next day.

LESSONS I LEARNED THE HARD WAY!
Don't ever assume someone is going to return your belongings the next day—or ever, for that matter!

It was frustrating to get to school the following morning and hear my friend say, "What? I thought I gave it back to you!" My mom's class ring was nowhere to be found. Of course my mother didn't get upset because she didn't know the ring was gone. I felt bad about losing it but thought, "Oh well. It was an old ring anyway—my mother has more valuable jewelry than that."

Three years later, as a senior in high school, it was time to get class rings. My schoolmates and I were beaming with pride as we displayed our "trophies." It was as if all we had accomplished in high school was symbolized in those rings. And then it hit me...*I lost my mother's class ring!* Until I had one of my own, I had no idea how precious a possession that ring truly was. It was a sinking feeling. There was no way to get my mother's ring back. The guilt was overwhelming.

And so it is with our virginity. When we're young and fancy-free, we don't necessarily grasp the value of having never entered into physical intimacy. Eventually, we give our virginity away to someone we trust relatively well, and we do so with scarcely enough thought. Just like my mother's class ring, we realize the next day that we can't get our virginity back, but even then, we may not be overly concerned. It's not until we meet the love of our life, that person who is to be our partner for all time, that we realize the magnitude of what we have lost. It is at that point that we also understand how, in giving ourselves to another lover, we let someone else have what belonged exclusively to our mate.

Think about it. **Your virginity can only be given to *one* person *one* time.** That makes it a very special gift! What a joy it is to give that gift to your soul mate as a celebration of your marriage commitment. On the other hand, what a disappointment to have to tell your spouse you already gave it away.

Simply put, *our virginity is valuable because our future mate is valuable.*

In closing, it's important to note that your virginity is something you can give away in a moment, but cannot take back for a lifetime. Furthermore, after having sex, the image of your nakedness will remain on the minds of the ones who beheld your unclothed body long after you put your clothes back on. You have a once-in-a-lifetime opportunity to save lovemaking, the most physically bonding activity two people can share, for the *one* and *only* person who deserves a gift of that magnitude—your future covenant partner! (Note: In Chapter Ten we'll answer the question, "What if I've already lost my virginity?")

In the following chapter, we'll address a very important question, "How far is going too far?" In the meantime, check out the Points to Ponder.

1. What do you imagine your future mate might be like? What are some qualities that are important to you?

✳ _____

_____

_____

2. Would you do something if you knew for a fact God did not want you to do it? Why or why not?

✳ _____

_____

_____

3. What does it mean to you that Jesus can identify with how you feel when you are tempted to sin?

✳ _____

_____

_____

4. Have you ever lost something valuable? How did it make you feel?

* _____

_____

_____

5. What would it mean to you if your future spouse told you he/she resisted having sex so that he/she could give his/her virginity to you on your wedding night? What if he/she said he/she didn't think you were worth the wait?

* _____

_____

_____

_____

6. If you had to, would you rather spend one night in a room overrun by cockroaches or spiders?

* _____

_____

_____

_____

7. Where do you think two young people who want to wait until marriage to have sex should draw the line with physical intimacy?

*_____

_____

_____

How far is going too far?

*F*oreplay. Making out. Fooling around. There's more than one term used to describe kissing, touching, rubbing, and doing everything excluding intercourse. My best friend in high school was always appalled and mortified at the term her mother repeatedly used—*heavy petting*.

No matter what we call it, it's imperative that we take a look at the varying degrees of physical activity in which young people commonly engage. Why is it important? Because of the "Off-Limits Sports Car" principle, of course!

The Off-Limits Sports Car Principle

Jason was just 15 years old when his dad pulled into the driveway with a gift for him, a brand new fire-engine-red

Mustang! (I know what you're thinking—why can't *my* dad be more like Jason's?) The thunderous rumbling engine sounded like the heavenly choir to Jason, and he could not wait to drive his black leather upholstered limited edition dream car. Unfortunately that's *exactly* what Jason had to do. He had to wait until he was 16 in order to get his driver's license and legally operate the vehicle, which was nearly one year away.

Jason's dad parked the turbo-powered beauty in the garage and warned him, "You're not to drive this car for any reason. I am going to put the keys away, and on your six-teenth birthday, you can have them." Jason agreed and soon spent every waking moment daydreaming about blowing out 16 birthday candles and blowing by traffic on the interstate in his glorious sports car!

Jason frequently went out into the garage to visit Sally—a name he thought suited his Mustang rather well. He would slide down into the driver's seat, grip the leather steering wheel, and take repeated deep breaths, savoring the distinct smell of leather and "new car." He loved sitting in the vehicle and imagining starting the engine...until one day, he did more than imagine.

His mom and dad were at some charity event that was to last late into the night, so Jason knew there was no chance of getting caught. He searched through his dad's junk drawer until at last, there were the shiny Mustang car keys! As he headed out to the garage, he assured himself, "Nothing bad can happen from turning the key and just listening to the rumble of the engine." And so he did, and it was an awesome experience—so awesome, in fact, that Jason soon began starting the engine every time his parents were gone. It wasn't until Ben came over that he considered taking the next step.

Jason's parents went out to dinner and a movie and Ben came over to stay the night. As was his custom, Jason headed out to the garage and revved the ear-pounding engine. In the passenger seat, Ben was blown away! "Hey Jason, why don't you just drive her to the end of the driveway?" Against his better judgment, Jason agreed. It was just a few feet but it felt like a monumental mile to Jason. With the keys safely back in his dad's dresser drawer, Jason was glad that he didn't chicken out!

LESSONS I LEARNED THE HARD WAY!
Cops seem to think there's a big difference between *intending* to get your driver's license and actually *having* your driver's license—go figure!

Do you know where this story is headed? Let's fast forward three weeks. Ben and Jason are cautiously driving around the block. Now let's jump ahead two months. Ben and Jason are cruising down the highway! Did I mention Sally was a convertible?

Most teens believe intercourse is the only thing that constitutes as sex and other sexual activities do not count.[1]

Jason had never experienced such a high—the radio blaring, the wind blazing through his hair, and the speedometer pushing 85 mph. What a blast!

The experience was so invigorating that Jason felt like he heard bells and whistles going off. It was a little puzzling, however, when Ben commented that he too heard bells and whistles. One glance in his rearview mirror and Jason's "I'm loving life" bubble popped! Those bells and whistles were police sirens!

Jason was busted. He knew he would not only be grounded for life, but felt sure he just lost his Mustang—his dad would never reward him with that car once he realized how untrustworthy he had been.

What Fooling Around and Off-Limits Sports Cars Have in Common

When Jason sat in his sports car and put the keys in the ignition for the first time, he had no intention of going any further than that. He was content with that experience and didn't feel the need to push the limits anymore. However, routinely starting the engine got him thinking about doing more, and with a little peer pressure, he found the courage. What Jason didn't understand was that every time he pushed the limits further, it only made him want to push the limits even more!

And so it is with fooling around. When we're holding hands with someone and exchanging occasional kisses on the cheek, we're not necessarily thinking about jumping into bed and having sex! What we usually desire is to simply take the next "baby step"—maybe a quick kiss on the lips. After we experience a few of those, we start dreaming about enjoying a nice long French kiss. Once we get that nice long French kiss, we yearn to be touched and caressed. Once we have a few "touchy-feely" sessions...well...jumping into bed and having sex starts to seem like a great idea! (Okay, maybe we know it's not a good idea but our pounding heart wants to do it anyway.)

It's amazing how quickly a young couple can go from modest affection to all-out sexual intercourse. So where is it a good idea to draw the line? Well, you have to make that decision for yourself, but before I throw out a few helpful ideas, let's answer this question:

What Is the Purpose of Foreplay?

Do you know that our bodies *physically react* to activities such as kissing, being touched, and feeling someone else's body? Our heart rate picks up, our breathing gets slow and heavy, and blood rushes to our reproductive parts. In a male, sperm cells begin mixing with other bodily secretions making his sperm conducive to swimming. During arousal, a woman secretes lubricating vaginal fluids in preparation for intercourse.

What is the body doing during foreplay? *Preparing to have sex!* Young person, write the following statement on your forehead and never wash it off. (Okay, you don't have to go that far, but please commit this point to memory and don't forget it!)

Foreplay prepares us physically, mentally, and emotionally to have sexual intercourse.

Couples may cite a variety of reasons why they personally participate in foreplay, but our bodies testify to an undeniable purpose of arousal—it gets two people ready to have sex! With this in mind, does it make sense to engage in foreplay, to get physically aroused, if you have no intention of having sexual intercourse? The obvious conclusion is *no*.

I've heard school counselors actually encourage students to explore intimate physical activities and just draw the line at sexual intercourse. They advocate experimenting with arousal. That's a recipe for disaster! All that does is throw logs on the raging fire of a young person's sexual appetite and make sexual intercourse nearly impossible to resist.

Getting aroused and then slamming on the brakes, which is to cease from physical activity when the body is prepared for sexual intercourse, causes physical discomfort and, in some cases, actual pain and illness. In his book, *Intended for Pleasure*, Ed Wheat describes the physical consequences males can expect in such cases:

> If there are repeated episodes of failure to ejaculate, especially following prolonged arousal periods, there can be some injury to the prostate gland, leading to a condition known as prostatitis.

This also occurs in men not yet married but engaged in prolonged petting. Symptoms include low-back pain, pelvic pressure, urethral discharge, and slight pain while urinating. The urine is usually free of infection, but the prostate is enlarged, sometimes tense and very tender.[2]

It's not just men who experience a physical backlash from ungratified sexual arousal. During foreplay, a woman experiences an increase in blood supply to her genitals, so much so that they swell to two to three times their normal size. (Totally freaky, I know!) During sexual intercourse, this increased blood supply helps to maximize the sensation of sexual climax, but when climax is never reached, a woman is left feeling uncomfortably bloated. She may also experience throbbing pain in her vaginal area for a couple of hours while waiting for the blood supply to subside.

Emotional Disadvantages of Fooling Around

Another major consequence of unquenched arousal is the *emotional* toll it takes on us. I often warn parents, if after spending time with a member of the opposite sex, your teenager is snippy with

78 percent of new cases of genital herpes were caused by a virus found chiefly in the mouths of 16- to 21-year-olds (i.e., acquired though oral sex).[3]

you, easily angered, and seemingly flustered and frustrated, it may be because he or she has been involved in foreplay.

Are you familiar with the term *sexually frustrated?* When people stir up their sexual appetites without satisfying their physical cravings (i.e., no sexual intercourse), they often become hostile, aggravated, and frustrated because of the emotional letdown and hormonal deluge they experience.

Simply put, it's not natural for the body to get ready to have sex and then not have it.

Are there other ways to achieve climax without having intercourse? Yes, but now we're blatantly looking for creative ways to get around God's boundaries for sex. Remember, we have no business enjoying the benefits of sexual gratification without the covenant commitment (review Chapter Two if need be).

Let me ask you a question. Do you want your future spouse pursuing alternatives to sexual intercourse that still allow him or her to experience sexual climax with a girlfriend or boyfriend? Of course you don't. As a general rule, if physical contact is causing sexual climax, two unmarried people have gone too far.

Just like the sight of a steak makes a hungry man salivate, foreplay makes a person desperate for sex. Even kissing can cause tremendous sexual

More than half of teens ages 15 to 19 say they've had oral sex.[4]

arousal. Knowing that sex is sacred and that fooling around prepares the body, mind, and emotions to have sex, I ask you again, what is the purpose of making out if you don't plan on having sex?

The truth is, fooling around does one of two things:

1. Sets us up for aggravation and disappointment because our intense desires go unmet

2. Sets us up to go all the way

Deciding Where to Draw the Line

When you are contemplating where you plan to draw the line with physical activity, please understand that the more liberty you give yourself, the more difficult you are actually making things. As a general rule, *the further we go, the further we **want** to go.* As we previously learned, when a couple increases their level of physical interaction, resisting sexual intercourse becomes more difficult. And what happens if a young lady is ready to stop but her boyfriend isn't?

A dear friend of mine fought back the tears while sharing her testimony with a group of high school girls. She explained that as a teenaged girl, she and an attractive young man were fooling

57 percent of rapes occur on a date.[5]

around one evening at his house while his parents were gone. She enjoyed the kissing and touching, but eventually felt that things were going too far. She told him she wanted to stop, but he refused to listen to her. With a horrifying forcefulness he proceeded to have intercourse with her, totally ignoring her objections. She lost her virginity, not because she was ready to give it away, but because an aroused young man was not willing to let his desires go unmet.

You see, it's not just about how far *you* can go and still resist having sex; your partner may insist you've gone too far to stop! When a man takes advantage of a woman under these circumstances, it's referred to as date rape. Even though it is unlawful, unfortunately it's extremely difficult to enforce legal consequences—if a guy insists it was mutual sex, how can a young lady prove otherwise?

Principles of Boundary Setting

You need to decide where you want to draw the line with physical activity *before* you find yourself in a passionate make-out session—once aroused, we tend to lose perspective. Furthermore, the more specific your boundaries are, the less chance there is for gray areas that lead to compromise. Once identified, these standards must be clearly communicated with whomever you are dating. If your boundaries are mocked, met with contempt, or rejected by someone you're dating, you have no business dating that person! If you and your honey are not in agreement about maintaining physical boundaries, it's just a matter of time before those boundaries are violated.

Some examples of boundaries two young people might commit to are:

* Kisses are "pecks" on the cheeks, not open mouth kisses on the lips.

* We never lay down together—we're upright at all times.

* Our hands do not touch private parts or "wander" around.

* We're never at each other's houses when parents aren't home.

* We don't hang out alone in the car; once we arrive at our destination, we get out.

To Kiss or Not to Kiss

Before I go on to the next step in the boundary setting process, allow me to address the issue of kissing. Kissing is something we tend to think nothing about, which is to say, we consider it a perfectly acceptable, if not an expected part of a dating relationship. However, a kiss can be very passionate, and can easily ignite sexual arousal. Traditionally, kissing is viewed as "no big deal," but in reality, can be quite an intimate, bonding experience. Knowing this, it's important that we do not simply follow the masses in this area. Sure, society will make fun of anyone who says he wants to wait until he is married to French kiss, but then again, society is being devastated by divorce, infidelity, STDs, and unwanted pregnancies—hardly the crowd we want to take advice from.

My point is that even though it can sound a bit extreme in our culture to say we don't want to kiss until we're married, it truly is a wise decision. Should you commit to save your kisses for your future spouse, it is a most admirable resolution. I, for one, feel very proud of any young person who holds to such an uncompromising standard.

Young person, you don't have to engage in passionate kissing just because it's socially acceptable. You have a choice, a wonderful opportunity to set your own standards based on your ideas about love and future romance.

Accountability: The Key to Keeping Boundaries

Identifying physical boundaries is one thing; keeping them is another. Ironically, determining off-limit intimacy levels can actually cause temptation to escalate! Experience tells us that "forbidden

87 percent of teens ages 12 through 19 say it would be easier to postpone sexual activity if they were able to have more open, honest conversations with parents.[6]

fruit" tends to provoke humanity's lust. (Remember Jason and his off-limits sports car?)

When faced with a wave of sexual longing, young couples often get swept off their feet, unexpectedly forsaking their boundary commitments. Due to inexperience, they underestimate temptation's powerful pull. How quickly it can engulf one's good intentions and promises! Furthermore, a drowning man is in no position to rescue the lady drowning next to him. *This is why third-party accountability is so important.*

Once you have clearly defined sexual boundaries, you should share your commitment with an outside source—a "lifeguard" of sorts who will keep an eye on your dating relationship (if you choose to date) and blow the whistle if things get out of hand. This person is not being nosey. On the contrary, he or she is empowered by you and the person you are dating to stay aware, informed, and connected to the relationship as a continual source of encouragement and accountability.

Should you find yourself tempted to compromise, you can go to your accountability partner for counsel and prayer. Also, you need an accountability partner who will approach you regularly and ask some forthright questions, such as, "How well are you two maintaining your physical boundaries?" "Have you been struggling lately?" "How much time are you two spending alone with each other?"

When we know we will give account for our actions to someone we admire and respect, it can throw a wet blanket on the fiery embers of temptation. Since we dread the thought of admitting we went back on our commitment, we become apprehensive in those crucial moments when we feel the urge to push past our physical boundaries. As a result, having an accountability partner can make all the difference in the moment of decision.

Every couple who chooses abstinence needs ongoing accountability, someone who will not only keep up with how the relationship is progressing emotionally, but will continually ask how things are going *physically,* in terms of maintaining their stated boundaries. This should not be a peer relationship, but rather, a mature, caring adult who will motivate you in your commitment.

If at all possible, I suggest that you ask one or both of your parents to fill this role in your life. If, for whatever reason, you are unable to look to your parents, perhaps there is another adult in your life who has integrity, godly character, and wisdom who can serve in this capacity for you (young men need male partners and young ladies need female partners). I strongly suggest that you have your accountability partner read my book *Choosing to Wait, A Guide to Inspiring Abstinence.* He or she will not only be given specific guidelines for serving as your accountability partner, but will also be brought up to speed with all the principles you and I have been learning throughout this study. (Log onto *LauraGallier.com* to purchase the book.)

So What Are You Waiting For?

Go ahead and take out a pen and paper and start writing out your physical boundaries. You may or may not be in a dating relationship right now, but either way, you need to make up your mind where you plan to draw the line. Then think and pray about who that special accountability partner can be. Make sure he or she gets a copy of your list.

Closing Remark

Your future mate is out there somewhere. Where do you desire that he or she draw the line with the opposite sex before you two meet? Should you have an equally high standard for yourself?

Points
to Ponder

1. In your own words, what is the purpose of foreplay?

*

_____

_____

2. Describe how it affects a young person's mood and emotions when he or she comes close to having sex but "slams on the brakes" (i.e., no sexual intercourse)?

*

_____

_____

3. In your opinion, does fooling around satisfy a couple's sexual longings? Why or why not?

*

_____

_____

4. Where do you specifically think it's wise to draw the line with physical activity?

✳ _____

_____

_____

5. Do you find these terms ironic: *jumbo shrimp, camping resort,* and *pretty ugly*?

✳ _____

_____

_____

6. Once a couple decides they don't want to have premarital sex, what are some practical ways they can guard against going too far?

✳ _____

_____

_____

Chapter Six

I could use some dating advice; got any?

I still remember when a boy passed me a note for the first time. I was in the fourth grade. I was staring at the back of Alan's head and thinking, "Wow, he's got a ton of hair gel in his hair," when suddenly he flung a tiny crumpled piece of paper over his shoulder onto my desk. I got that "deer in the headlights" wide-eyed look as I stared at the balled-up note! What in the world did Alan have to say to *me*?

Like a seasoned detective, I started the covert operation of unfolding the handwritten masterpiece, all the while cleverly keeping one eye peeled toward Mrs. Wilson's desk. There in smeared pencil were the radiant words, "*I think U R cute. Will U go with me? Check One.*" The bottom of the note had three checkboxes to choose from: *Yes, No, Maybe.*

I had an overinflated idea of what it would be like to have a boyfriend, so without hesitation, I checked the "Yes" box and wrote, "Thank U. I will go with U." (If my memory serves me correctly, I drew an eyeball in place of the "I".)

Even though I agreed to "go with" Alan, we never went anywhere. We just saw each other at school and communicated via airborne note. I thought everything was going quite well—that is until the day Alan called me out to the soccer field during recess. Right there in front of his friends and mine he announced, "I want to break up with you." All heads turned toward me, at which point I asked, "Why?" All heads turned back to Alan and he proceeded to say the words that would sting long after the moment passed— "Because you're ugly!"

I was new at the guy-girl thing but quickly learned that relationships with the opposite sex could be both exciting and painful. From that moment on, I had no desire to toss sweet notes onto Alan's desk; I did, however, have visions of chunking a live grenade!

Remind Me Why I'm Getting Dating Advice From You?

Okay, that's how it went down with Alan in the fourth grade, but remember, that was a long time ago. I've done a lot of living since then, and I've learned some very important lessons along the way in regards to dating. I'm going to share some tips with you, but first, let's make sure we're on the same page about the definition of dating.

Dating, in its simplest form, refers to a guy and a girl getting to know each other. *The pivotal factor here is the degree that we choose to get to know a member of the opposite sex.*

You see, intimacy occurs when we give someone access to the most personal, vulnerable aspects of who we are. In intimate relationships, we give *ourselves* to others. Furthermore, the more intimate our premarital relationships are (emotionally and physically), the more of ourselves we give away.

The danger of our culture's current dating trend is that it encourages young people to hold nothing back, to totally give themselves physically and emotionally to whomever they are dating at the time—as if, by some miracle boomerang effect, our acts of vulnerability will be returned to us when the relationship ends. In reality, each failed intimate relationship makes a significant withdrawal from our soul, which can bankrupt us long before we ever enter into marriage. As our soul "account" dwindles, so does our ability to freely trust, love, forgive, and commit to someone for life.

Now, let's not overlook the fact that it can be advantageous to get socially acquainted with the opposite sex. As guys and gals, when we cultivate

"Teenage 'dating' websites that boast millions of members encourage teenage patrons to select not prom dates but partners for casual sexual escapades."[1]

friendships with each other, it helps us understand and relate to how "the other half" lives. It also gives us a glimpse of the qualities we do and do not want in a mate someday. However, this does not mean we should pursue *serious commitments* with one member of the opposite sex after another, which has few benefits, if any, and a myriad of possible negative consequences.

As with most of life's issues, *the key to dating is balance.* Since our culture's dating practices are so very out of balance, it is imperative that we take an objective look at the subject. By objective, I mean we must be willing to compare worldly dating trends with God's wisdom and standards.

We do not want to totally isolate ourselves from the opposite sex, nor do we want to be entangled in overly intimate relationships. Here are some practical ways to keep relationships with the opposite sex balanced:

1. Don't start dating too early.

Throughout the Bible book Song of Solomon, we are repeatedly warned not to stir up or awaken love until it pleases, meaning it is not wise to prematurely incite our desire for romance or sex. Having said that, nothing, and I stress, *not one good thing*, comes from dating when we are young teens—13,

14, or 15. Sixteen may very well be too young also, depending on our individual maturity level.

It's one thing to attend a co-ed supervised social function with a group of friends, but two smitten middle school kids have no business going to the movies alone (or anywhere else for that matter)! Even as freshmen and sophomores in high school, most of us lack the maturity to handle the pressures and emotions that accompany dating relationships.

For those young teens who are anxious to start dating, may I lovingly remind you that God has a mate in mind for you to spend the *rest of your life* with—surely it is a waste of time and energy to start actively looking for this person a decade or so before we are even ready for marriage!

"Who said anything about finding a mate? I just want to have a good time!" If that's how you feel, go rent a movie with your buddies, enjoy a large milkshake with your best friend, or try sliding down the stairs in silky pajama pants with your siblings, but don't pursue dating too early in life. Cultivating healthy dating relationships requires that we have the maturity to set and maintain some very important boundaries—why not give ourselves some time before we take on this responsibility?

25 percent of girls and 30 percent of boys have sex by age 15; 21 percent of 9th graders have slept with four or more partners.[3]

LESSONS I LEARNED THE HARD WAY!
Sun tanning is a great way to pass the hours when you and
your friends are bored during the summer, but know this:

1. It may seem like sun tanning on the roof of your house will get you closer to the sun, and there-fore, produce a better tan, but it actually doesn't make a difference.

2. If you do choose to suntan on a roof and the roof is slanted, don't cover yourself in baby oil and then lay out on aluminum foil.

3. Sliding down shingles is painful!

---

2. Keep dating relationships casual.

Just as an inheritance gained in haste does not last very long, relationships formed through premature intimacy and rushed commitments are not equipped to stand the test of time, either. Unfortunately, young people these days tend to think of relationships with the opposite sex as an "all or nothing" proposition. As a result, teenagers tend to be mere acquaintances with certain members of the opposite sex or wrapped up in serious, all-consuming, committed relation-ships—there is very little middle ground.

> "An inheritance quickly gained at the beginning will not be blessed at the end." (Proverbs 20:21)

Premature sexual activity, increased jealousy and insecurities, Hollywood's deceptive influence, and our culture's tendency toward impatience are all likely factors that contribute toward teens' rushed commitments. In such cases, young people miss out on a major benefit of the single years—*the opportunity to cultivate quality friendships with members of the opposite sex without the entanglement of serious commitments.*

We can spend time with an attractive member of the opposite sex in social settings, enjoy having lunch together at school, and talk on the phone now and then, but it is not beneficial in the long run to spend every waking moment consumed with the relationship!

You need to know that it *is* possible to get to know a member of the opposite sex without making a serious commitment. You don't have to pursue deep levels of emotional and physical connection simply because that's the expectation and norm these days.

Furthermore, just because someone has caught our eye does not mean we need to pursue a dating relationship with him or her, and just because we are attracted to someone does not mean we have to take that relationship to the next level. In actuality, we can appreciate the way someone looks without taking any action at all!

Early sexual experiences correlate with depression and drug use."[4]

You Betta Back Off, Girl—
That's *My* Man!

I always think it's sad when I see teenagers expending all of their energy making sure their girlfriend or boyfriend is not looking at someone else, and that no one else is checking out *their man* (or *their girl*). I often ask young people, "What's the purpose of committing to be an exclusive couple, avoiding all other members of the opposite sex, when you are too young to pursue marriage?" Often motivated by jealousy and insecurity, this sort of "forsake all others" commitment usually creates a variety of problems (also known as *drama*). He anxiously wonders, *Why was my girlfriend walking with Johnny after third period yesterday?* She worries, *Is it true that Sally told Jenny that Amy saw Jessica and my boyfriend exchange phone numbers on the bus this morning?*

Teenaged committed relationships are often an exhausting rollercoaster of emotional ups and downs because the relationship is in a "limbo" of sorts. The two teens are like a married couple in some ways, but not in others. They have the same monogamous standard and protective jealousy as married couples, yet lack the assurance and security that married people enjoy—a lifelong commitment signified through marriage vows. A tough day, a misunderstood note, an attractive new student in science class, and suddenly the relationship is in jeopardy!

Such relationships are exhausting and can suck all the fun out of our teen years, the time when we should be meeting all kinds of interesting people and having a blast with friends, who, by the way, often fall to the wayside when a boyfriend or girlfriend enters the scene.

I'm not advocating a philosophy that says, "Commit to no one; just play the field and go from one person to the next." I'm talking about staying on the sidelines altogether. We shouldn't isolate ourselves from the opposite sex, but we don't need to fill up our lives with them, either. Keep it simple! Keep it casual!

3. Don't isolate.

As previously mentioned, young people often neglect their family relationships and friendships once a boyfriend or girlfriend comes along. They spend every waking moment with their "sweetie," isolating themselves from other key relationships in their lives. As a result, their priorities begin spiraling out of control. I've seen situations where a young person's spiritual commitments, grades, friendships, and extracurricular activities take a drastic plunge because he or she is so focused on a love interest.

> *"A man who isolates himself seeks his own desire; he rages against all wise judgment"* (Proverbs 18:1 NKJV).

Hey, do me a favor. Get out a piece of paper and make a list. Write down your lifetime priorities in order from greatest to least. (What is most important to you right now? What goals do you have?) Go ahead, make your list, and then keep reading.

Now, if you are not dating anyone at this time, fold the piece of paper and stick it in the back of this book—should you start seeing someone, get your list out and then follow the instructions provided in the following paragraph.

If you are currently dating someone, take a serious look at your list of priorities and ask yourself, "Are my priorities suffering as a result of my dating relationship?" If the answer is *yes*, you need to make some adjustments. This is a great time to get some advice from your parents—*yes, I went there!* They may wear dorky shoes and fall asleep before your night even gets started on the weekends, but you have to give them some credit—they survived the teen years that you are just now entering. The key is to come up with some tangible boundaries that will help you maintain your life's priorities and live a balanced life, and your parents (or accountability partner as described in the last chapter) can be a huge help with this process!

I strongly encourage you *not* to neglect your friends as a result of focusing too much time, energy, and attention on a girlfriend or boyfriend.

When polled, 49 percent of teens said their parents influenced their decisions about sex most strongly.[6]

Chances are, you and your "honey" will break up someday—I know you don't believe me, but it's true! When that happens, you'll wish you had not run off all of your friends. In all honesty, buddies don't usually come back around too easily after being disregarded for a girl (or guy).

If you choose to have a boyfriend or girlfriend, it's beneficial to go out in groups and spend time in social settings involving your friends *and* your date. Having friends around helps keep us out of physically compromising situations and also gives us a better idea of what kind of person we're dating. If he or she can't stand our friends, the people we love to hang around, perhaps we are not going to be compatible with that person in the long run.

4.   Guard your heart.

Have you ever met someone who seemed like his life was out of control? We often say of that kind of person, "He's got issues!" The Bible tells us where our *issues* come from—the heart (mind, will, and emotions), which is why we have to diligently protect it. The emphasis of this book is about guarding our bodies from premature sexual activity, but the Bible also warns us to guard our *hearts*.

> *"Keep* [guard] *your heart with all diligence, for out of it spring the issues of life"* (Proverbs 4:23 NKJV).

If I've seen it once, I've seen it a hundred times. A young girl experiences mutual attraction, and starts spending more

"Even if a baby of a teen mother is born healthy, he or she is still likely to experience numerous complications later on, including poor health; inadequate education; low intelligence; and anger at his or her family, community, and society."[7]

and more time with a handsome young man. At first, their conversations are about silly things and are peppered with giggles and sighs. But in time, they both start opening up and sharing more personal things—past hurts, current fears, future dreams and aspirations. As they trust each other with their most vulnerable memories, thoughts, and feelings, powerful bonds of intimacy are formed.

Eventually, a falling out occurs and the couple splits up. Unfortunately, they have no way of taking back the emotional investment they made in each other. In such cases, the pain of breaking up is devastating for young people and can negatively affect their grades, friendships, sleep patterns, eating habits, and other significant aspects of their lives.

Another incentive to guard our hearts is that when we make strong emotional connections with members of the opposite sex, physical temptation intensifies. However, even if two young people manage to protect their relationship from *physical* intimacy, they still run the risk of forming damaging "soul ties" based on an overabundance of *emotional* intimacy. Soul ties are the mental and emotional strings that keep us connected to someone long after we have parted ways.

I have counseled ladies over the years who are married, have a house full of children, but live with nagging feelings of attachment toward certain men from their past. Particular songs, scents, or familiar settings can trigger a flood of memories and emotions. In those moments, a woman desires more than anything to somehow connect with the man she bonded with in her youth.

While soul ties can be a surefire recipe for infidelity, they are also a source of ongoing torment as men and women struggle to overcome the mental and emotional battles when memories of "old flames" ignite. And consider how hurtful it is for a spouse to learn that his or her mate has recurring feelings for someone else! It undermines the foundation of trust on which relationships are built.

Abstinence is just as much about saving our hearts for our future mates as it is about saving our bodies. I strongly encourage you to guard your heart and protect yourself from emotions and experiences that can ultimately cause regret and anguish. To reiterate a point made earlier, when we share our heart with someone, in essence, we are giving ourselves away. Just like we can't un-ring a bell, we can't undo the emotional intimacy we create with someone. This is another reason why dating relationships should be kept casual.

"In the United States in 2005, about half of all teenagers had sexual intercourse by age 16 (or the eleventh grade)."[8]

5. Don't get caught up in missionary dating!

We've all seen it, if not lived it. Some sweet girl with a big heart and naive mind latches on to a down-and-outer. "He needs my help," she tells concerned loved ones. In an effort to rehabilitate him, she stays in the relationship even though it revolves almost entirely around him and his constant needs. She holds onto the hope that her love will somehow change him. Time drags on and everyone *except her* sees the writing on the wall—he's taking advantage of her good intentions and dragging her down with him.

> *Do not be unequally yoked together with unbelievers*
> (2 Corinthians 6:14 NKJV).

I've also seen situations where young men get all wrapped up with "needy" girlfriends.

Dating someone in an effort to somehow modify his or her behavior is often referred to as "missionary dating." I've noticed that Christian kids can be especially susceptible to this. I could give this book away for free if I had a nickel for every time a young girl started her conversation with me by saying, "I'm a Christian and I'm trying to get my boyfriend to accept Christ." Guys do the same thing. They think God is calling them to date a girl in order to influence her spiritual beliefs and win her to the Lord.

Did you know that Scripture actually warns against this? Second Corinthians 6:14 tells us not to be unequally yoked with unbelievers. Upon hearing this passage, we tend to envision egg yolk and wonder what in the world this Scripture means. Actually, that's not the kind of "yoke" God is referring to here. He's talking about the harness placed around two animals' necks, like oxen for example, used to keep them side by side while they plow up and down a field. This binding yoke forces two animals to take the same path.

When God tells us not to be unequally yoked, He's telling us not to join ourselves in a committed relationship with an unbeliever. Our Master (God) has a path for us to travel and we don't want to hook up with someone who isn't ready or willing to go in the direction where we are called. With this in mind, we have no business entering into romantic relationships in an effort to help or change someone.

One quality missionary daters tend to have in common is they truly believe that they are the *only* hope their boyfriend or girlfriend has. They are convinced that if they break off the relationship, their needy companion will spiral out of control. In this way, missionary daters suffer from false guilt, wrongly concluding that the other person's well-being, future, and perhaps eternal destination, are dependent on their own ability

"Throughout puberty, bodies add bone, redistribute weight, and gain height, while the inner organs (including the uterus) mature. Pregnancy interferes with this, because another set of hormones directs the body to sustain new life. Nature protects the fetus, which may take essential nutrients (especially calcium and iron) from the mother. If normal pubescent growth is deflected, that causes the girl to become a shorter and sicker woman than she otherwise would have been."[9]

to love, care, and transform that person. This is a deceptive lie!

A troubled young man doesn't need the mentorship of a girlfriend; he needs a godly man in his life. Along those same lines, a distressed young lady doesn't need a boyfriend to coach her through her issues. She needs a mature spiritual mother to come along and minister to her. God knows this and is well able to orchestrate a plan that involves bringing the right people along at the right time. We don't need to "help God" by attempting to rescue members of the opposite sex though the avenue of dating relationships.

WHAT'S THE POINT IN GETTING MARRIED
when a couple can just move in together? Keep reading.
We'll discuss this in an upcoming chapter!

It's easier for someone to push us off a stool than it is for us to pull someone up onto a stool with us. Likewise, missionary daters are much more likely to be negatively influenced by their troubled counterpart than they are to actually motivate lasting change in their boyfriend or girlfriend.

Simply stated, *if someone is not healthy spiritually and emotionally, end the dating relationship immediately.*

In teens that report having been sexually intimate, only about half of their parents believed their teens had gone beyond kissing.[10]

6. Protect dating relationships from physical activity.

Just as I started to type this section's subtitle, I was interrupted and took a break from writing—the reason is slightly ironic. A distraught young lady called to tell me that she and her boyfriend of six months just broke up. The reason? They have not been respecting each other's boundaries, and have gone too far physically. It's taken a terrible toll on the relationship. Instead of the lighthearted fun this Christian couple used to enjoy together, they are now plagued by stress, guilt, confusion, and resentment toward each other. As a result, he called this morning to tell her that he can't continue the relationship, leaving her full of regret and disappointment.

The break-up prompted this young lady to have an honest and open talk with her parents, during which she confessed everything she had been doing in the relationship. Her parents have now committed to take a more active role providing boundaries and accountability for their daughter in the future, which is great. Still, the lesson is clear—if you want to take a perfectly good relationship and ruin it, just disregard God's sexual standards. For the many reasons stated throughout this book, premarital sexual activity is not wise, even if it's just "fooling around."

Speaking of dating, ever wonder if your dating relationship is healthy? Take some time to reflect on the Points to Ponder and then take the quiz on the following page.

Points to Ponder

1. In your opinion, what are some benefits of building friendships with the opposite sex?

*_____

_____

_____

2. What is the purpose of committing to be an exclusive couple, avoiding all other members of the opposite sex, when you are too young to pursue marriage?

*_____

_____

_____

3. If you noticed that your science teacher had a fabric softener sheet stuck to the back of her skirt, would you tell her?

*_____

_____

_____

4. In your opinion, why might it be necessary to guard your heart in a dating relationship?

✳ _____

_____

_____

5. Would you date someone who is not a Christian? Why or why not?

✳ _____

_____

_____

Quiz

"Is my dating relationship healthy?"

SECTION ONE

Put a check if you and the person you're seeing...

_____ Have fun together most of the time.

_____ Each enjoy spending time separately with your own friends, as well as with each other's friends.

_____ Always feel safe with each other.

_____ Trust each other.

_____ Are faithful to each other (if you have made this commitment).

_____ Support each other's individual goals in life, like ministry, education, or career goals.

_____ Respect each other's opinions, even when they are different.

_____ Solve conflicts without putting each other down, cursing at each other, or making threats.

_____ Enjoy spiritually beneficial conversations that center around the truth of God's Word.

_____ Both accept responsibility for your actions.

_____ Both apologize when you're wrong.

_____ Both have decision-making power in the relationship.

_____ Are proud to be with each other.

_____ Encourage each other's interests like sports and leisure activities.

_____ Have some privacy—your letters, journals, and personal phone calls are respected as your own.

_____ Have close friends and relatives who are happy about your relationship.

_____ Never feel like you're being pressured for sex.

_____ Always allow each other "space" when you need it.

_____ Always treat each other with respect.

SECTION TWO

Put a check if one of you:

_____ Gets extremely jealous or accuses the other of cheating or wanting to cheat.

_____ Puts the other down by calling names, cursing, or making the other feel bad about him or herself.

_____ Yells or speaks in harsh tones.

_____ Doesn't take the other person, or things that are important to him/her, seriously.

_____ Doesn't listen when the other talks.

_____ Frequently criticizes the other's friends or family.

_____ Pressures the other for sex.

_____ Has ever threatened to hurt the other or commit suicide if the other leaves.

_____ Cheats or threatens to cheat.

_____ Is into pornography.

_____ Tells the other how to dress.

_____ Is opposed to or makes fun of the other's commitment to Christ or involvement with church.

_____ Acts one way at church but another way outside of church.

_____ Has ever grabbed, pushed, hit, or physically hurt the other.

_____ Blames the other for his or her own behavior ("If you hadn't made me mad, I wouldn't have—").

_____ Embarrasses or humiliates the other.

_____ Smashes, throws, or destroys things.

_____ Tries to keep the other from having commitments and ambitions, such as a job or education goals.

_____ Makes all the decisions about what the two of you do.

_____ Tries to make the other feel crazy or plays mind games.

_____ Goes back on promises and regularly does not keep his/her word.

_____ Acts controlling or possessive.

_____ Uses alcohol or drugs.

_____ Ignores or withholds affection as a way of punishing the other.

_____ Depends completely on the other to meet social or emotional needs.

CONCLUSION

Lots of checks in Section One and no checks in Section Two:

It seems that your relationship has healthy qualities. If the relationship continues for another three months, take the quiz again and see if the results have changed any.

Some or no checks in Section One and one or more checks in Section Two:

You need to immediately seek input from your parents or a qualified caring adult concerning your relationship. It appears to be lacking the qualities of a healthy relationship and has the potential to be harmful to you. Please take this warning seriously! Unhealthy dating relationships are not something to ignore.

Chapter Seven

What are some common objections and rebuttals concerning abstinence?

*I*t's strange to think that a broken clock tells the correct time twice a day, isn't it? No matter where the hour and minute hands get stuck, they display the accurate time for sixty seconds every morning and again every afternoon. Similarly, it is possible for certain opinions, philosophies, and views to initially appear wise and correct, only to find that when actually acted upon in life, they are broken theories that don't really work.

In this chapter, we will examine the most common arguments people make in an effort to undermine premarital abstinence. Just so you know, I don't get all uptight or wig-out when my views are mocked or challenged, and I encourage you not to either.

I'm not advising that you ignore your critics—our convictions are strengthened when we contemplate and respond to skeptics' arguments. At the same time, we don't need to exhaust ourselves defending our stance. It is God, not us, who ultimately has the ability to transform a person. Take it from me, yelling and losing your temper in an effort to convince someone God is good and His ways are best doesn't go over so well!

The following objections are based primarily on simple logic versus spiritual understanding due to the fact that anyone who asserts such claims is failing to discern the spiritual implications of sex in the first place.

Objection #1:

I don't want to marry someone until I know if we're sexually compatible.

Sex is an integral part of any marriage, but it is *not* the most important thing. Furthermore, there are many other factors besides sex that determine long-term compatibility with a spouse, such as spiritual maturity, family ideology, lifetime aspirations, and common social and recreational interests—just to name a few. It's not everyday that we meet someone who is compatible in these crucial areas. Does it make any sense that upon finding a unique love match based on these vitally important

"Many STDs have no symptoms but severe consequences."[1]

factors, we would then dump that person because we feel they could have performed better in bed?

Of course, we all want to have exciting sex lives with our spouses, but research proves that most couples actually have to work at their sexual compatibility, versus having some innate chemistry that keeps their sexual connection steamy and passionate over the years. Believe it or not, it was my grandmother who once told me, "There are worse things than sex to have to practice over and over until you get it just right." You know, she makes a valid point!

We don't need to physically try someone out to decide if we want to spend the rest of our lives with him or her. If our spiritual and emotional connections are there, and we possess a strong sense of attraction toward that special someone, we can rest assured that the physical connection will be there too once we're married (even if we have to practice a bit)!

Objection #2:

I need to be sexually experienced so I'll know how to satisfy my spouse someday.

While all women have the same reproductive anatomy, as do men, each individual has different preferences when it comes to physical touch and lovemaking. As a result, we have no business "learning" how to please our mate from anyone *but our mate*. Furthermore, I would hardly be impressed if my husband caressed me a certain way because that's how his ex-girlfriend liked to be touched!

Suppose your future mate was somehow able to contact you right now and have a short conversation with you. Which would you rather hear her (or him) say?

(a) "Oh, sweetheart! I can't wait to meet you! In the meantime, you'll be glad to know I've been doing all kinds of sexual acts and favors for my boyfriend. This way I'll be prepared to seduce and satisfy you someday. He's teaching me a variety of useful techniques. I'll know exactly how to please you when we get married because I've been pleasing guys for years!"

(b) "Oh sweetheart! I can't wait to meet you! In the meantime, I've been focusing my attention on Christ and growing in spiritual wisdom and maturity. There have been times I have been tempted to give my heart and body to someone else, but I chose not to because I sincerely believe you are worth waiting for. It's not always easy to wait, but I know it will all be worth it when you and I give ourselves to each other as husband and wife."

Conclusion: *There's absolutely nothing romantic or impressive about getting sexually experienced in preparation to please one's future spouse!*

Objection #3:

It's okay to have sex as long as I am engaged or planning to marry the person someday.

Would you let someone operate on you who says he plans to be a doctor in the future? How about if he just got accepted into medical school—would that provide enough credibility for you to allow him to remove your appendix? Of course not! We know that until a person walks across the stage, receives his or her diploma, and officially graduates from medical school with a doctorate, he or she is no doctor!

And so it is with marriage. Hoping to get married, making plans to get married, even wearing an engagement ring as a promise of getting married someday is *not* the same thing as *being* married. Furthermore, *intending* on committing to someone for life is not equivalent to *having* committed to someone for life.

For young people who insist there's nothing wrong with having sex with someone as long as they plan to marry the person, I have a fun and effective assignment that helps expose the fallacy of their thinking. I encourage them to ask ten adults, "In your past, was there ever anyone you sincerely believed you would marry, perhaps even became engaged to, but who you didn't end up marrying

Over 50 percent of teens ages 15 to 17 that had sex believed they would marry their first sexual partner.[2]

after all?" Almost all grownups have a story about a person they thought for sure they would marry, but the relationship actually never progressed to that point. Many people have testimonies of going as far as getting engaged to someone, only to break up with their fiancé and forgo marriage for one reason or another.

The conclusion is obvious—planning to marry someone can't possibly be the factor that makes sex "okay" because there is no way to know if we really will marry someone until we are, in fact, married.

Objection #4:

It's not realistic to wait until I'm married to have sex.

In today's society, teenagers often wonder if it is possible to be in their twenties, much less thirties or forties, and still be a virgin. They worry, "What if I don't get married until I'm 35 and I have to stay a virgin until then?"

It's no wonder young people feel this way. It seems most of society scoffs at preserving one's virginity. In the last decade, Hollywood has released several blockbuster movies that derive their plot out of making fun of a virgin. Until he has illicit intercourse at the conclusion of the movie, he is the subject of ridicule, humiliation, and scorn.

More than one of these movies involves high school students striving to lose their virginity before graduation. Such films lead students to believe they are social outcasts and failures if they don't "score" in their teens. What a cruel lie!

The truth is *it's actually unrealistic not to wait until we're married to start having sex!* Allow me to explain.

HOW DO I FIGURE OUT WHO GOD WANTS ME TO MARRY?
Keep reading! I'll answer this in an upcoming chapter.

Our physical bodies have three primary appetites: eating, sleeping, and having sex. All three of these appetites have something in common—they are insatiable, meaning we cannot satisfy them once and for all. Think about it. No matter how much we eat today or how full we get, tomorrow we will get hungry all over again. And no matter how much sleep we get tonight, tomorrow night our bodies will be weary and ready to sleep again. And so it is with sex. Just because we have sex once doesn't mean we don't want to have sex again, and therein lies the problem.

When young people start having sex with a girlfriend or boyfriend, they regularly satisfy their sexual appetites. But what happens when they break up? Who is going to satisfy their sexual cravings then? Are they just going to look for someone willing to have sex? Oftentimes the answer to this question is *yes,* creating a destructive lifestyle of promiscuity.

Unlike eating and sleeping, we don't *have* to engage our sexual appetites. Sure, we'll deal with ongoing cravings, but the moment we intentionally feed that appetite through sexual activity, those cravings escalate! Why not keep our sexual appetites under wraps until marriage, at which point we can have sex as often as we want for the most part? Whereas sex outside of marriage leaves a person vulnerable to "feast or famine" sexual encounters, marriage is basically a feast for life!

Suppose we are not going to meet and marry our mate until we are 25 years old. Then why start having sex at 17 years of age, or even 21, for that matter? Who is going to satisfy that appetite for the next 4 or 8 years? Better to "let it sleep" than to wake up your sexual appetite without a life-long sexual partner.

Myths Concerning Premarital Abstinence

Myth #1—Masturbation is a great way to satisfy one's sexual longings while remaining abstinent until marriage.

Masturbation is the act of sexually stimulating oneself. It requires that we experience the most physically intimate act two people can share (sexual gratification) all alone. The ironic thing about masturbation is that although it promises to temporarily satisfy our sexual desires, it only intensifies our longing for sex. Like a drug addict, we eventually become enslaved to the thing that we originally believed would serve us and meet our perceived needs.

For the person who desires a sexually pure life free from the guilt, addiction, and tormenting lust accompanied by perversion, you want to stay away from masturbation for the following valid reasons:

A. Masturbation does not satisfy, but instead, intensifies our longings for sex.

Let's face it, while masturbating, one is hardly imagining fluffy bunny rabbits hopping through a field of wildflowers. No, one must entertain sexually graphic thoughts in order to produce sexual feelings. In conjuring up and meditating on such sexually illicit and stimulating images, we intensely turn up the heat on our sexual appetites, which only makes our sexual cravings all the worse. As a result, it becomes nearly impossible to look at someone we find attractive without envisioning having sex with him or her because our minds are dominated by lust. This makes it very difficult to cultivate healthy relationships with members of the opposite sex and quickly becomes a source of torment.

B. What is supposed to connect us intimately to another instead leaves us feeling utterly alone.

Immediately after masturbating, reality confronts us—we were not ravished by a lover; we merely stimulated ourselves. This sober realization leaves us emotionally unsatisfied by the experience, making us more desperate for sexual intimacy, which drives us right back to masturbation. What a vicious cycle!

Loneliness is like a cloud of depression that hovers over one's head, continually overshadowing the joy and contentment we long for. It has been my experience in counseling young people who are involved in masturbation that they tend to battle extreme feelings of loneliness. This is no mystery to me. *You can't experience the most bonding physical act (sex) all by yourself without feeling utterly lonely as a result.* ***It's better to resist occasional sexual urges than to masturbate and evoke relentless feelings of loneliness!***

C. Masturbation is addicting.

I remember how confused I was the first time a lady friend of mine confided in me that she caught her husband masturbating. I wondered, *Why would he masturbate when he could have "real" sex with his wife?* I have since learned that masturbation often becomes a relentless addiction, in some cases compelling people to masturbate several times in a single day!

Since masturbation is based on fantasy and not reality, and involves intense meditation, people often become addicted to the mental and emotional escape that accompanies the act. The sexual scenario they've created in their minds becomes more appealing than reality, often causing such people to prefer masturbation over actual intercourse with their spouse. This "out of touch with reality" means of existence makes a person vulnerable to all kinds of rash behaviors, illogical decisions, and mental and emotional breakdowns. If a person is married, his addiction stands as a huge intimacy barrier between his spouse and him, which causes the marriage to break down.

D. Masturbation is self-centered, which is the essence of sin.

Just as we discussed in Chapter Three, all sin has its origin in self-centeredness. Sexual gratification was created to be *given to us* by someone else (i.e., their anatomy stimulates ours, resulting in sexual climax). By stimulating ourselves, we are taking an act that is meant to be a give-and-take experience between two people and reducing it to a self-motivated (self-centered) experience. What's more, we are imagining having sex with someone who is not our mate, and in this way we are guilty of adultery and/or fornication (see Matt. 5:28).

Myth #2—There's no point in getting married; two people who are in love can just move in together.

I am truly troubled by the number of people who are now choosing to forgo marriage and live together. In 2003, 9.2 million men and women lived together in unmarried-partner households.[4] Two primary reasons people choose to cohabitate are as follows:

1. People consider marriage irrelevant.

Young people want to know, "Does a ring on my finger and a signed marriage license really matter?" In light of our nation's current divorce rate, many young people see marriage as a useless ritual, an old tradition that need not be practiced in the future. I must concede that if one perceives marriage to be nothing more than an expensive wedding, exchange of rings, and a piece of paper filed with the county clerk, it does seem a bit ridiculous. However, *marriage is so much more than these things!* **It is a lifetime covenant commitment to one person witnessed by God Himself.**

As we've discussed in previous chapters, marriage is God's idea, not man's. We have incorporated traditions like garters and grooms' cakes, but let us not lose sight of the essence of marriage and its relevance—*two lives joined as one for life!* Building families without lifelong commitments is like building a house on the sand; it will never have the kind of stability and security that we, and our children, deserve and desire.

Perhaps you are afraid of a lifetime commitment because you have grown up amidst our nation's plague of divorce. You've seen how painful and costly divorces are and are leery of making yourself vulnerable to a marital split. Sometimes we falsely conclude that by not marrying our significant other, and simply moving in together instead, we will not suffer the consequences of divorce. However, this is not true.

Anytime we share a life together with someone by cohabitating* with them, break-ups are painful and costly. And when the only prerequisite for staying together is that we are a happy-go-lucky couple all of the time, as is often the case with cohabitation, we know it's just a matter of time

Married people are healthier than other adults. [5]

before a split occurs. All long-term relationships entail "peeks and valleys" and require ongoing compromise, sacrifice, and perseverance in order to survive.

✳COHABITATE:
To live with a lover outside of marriage.

Consider the following:

"In more recent years, a large proportion of young people began living together soon after the onset of dating, with little intention of remaining together permanently, and even less of getting married. Breaking up then becomes much more difficult than if couples had simply continued to date each other."[7]

Does a marriage license ensure a couple will stay together for life? No. **However, two people embracing a *covenant commitment* with one another and building their relationship on the principles in God's Word is quite a different matter.**

Couples that possess a fear of lifetime commitments are doomed from the start because quality relationships cannot exist on a foundation of fear, but rather, require trust.

2. People assume their marriage will be stronger if they live together first.

Research clearly proves that this philosophy is false. Couples who live together before marrying have nearly an *80 percent higher divorce rate* than those who do not![8] Furthermore, over half of the couples who cohabitate split up within five years.[9] That's not all. Studies show the following:

✳ Couples who had cohabitated had less positive problem-solving behaviors and were, on average, less supportive of each other than those who had not cohabitated.[10]

✳ Couples who had cohabitated before marriage had much higher rates of premarital violence than those who had not lived together. This premarital violence then leads to higher rates of marital violence, another factor related to divorce.[11]

✳ Those who cohabitate are generally more approving of divorce as a solution to marital problems.[12]

✳ A propensity to cohabitate soon after starting a romantic relationship leads to a pattern of instability. People who go through a series of *de facto* relationships are more likely to contract quick marriages, which are more vulnerable to unfaithfulness.[13]

✳ In the 1970s, about 60 percent of couples living together went on to marry their partners within three years. By the early 1990s, this figure dropped to about 35 percent.[14]

Why Buy the Cow?

You've probably heard the crude, yet fundamentally sound, cliché, "Why buy the cow when you can get the milk for free?" The truth is, we have no business living with someone, giving him access to everything in our lives that is sacred, without a commitment from him that assures he will love, honor, and cherish us for life (guys, the same is true for you). And certainly *kids* deserve this level of security from their parents!

On the occasions when people defend the validity of living with their partner instead of getting married, I challenge their stance by asking, "I understand *you* approve of that lifestyle, but are you at all familiar with how our nation's *children* feel about it?" I then encourage them to go interview a dozen elementary age children who are dealing with live-in boyfriends or the absence of one of their parents, and see how they feel about casually committed relationships. Most people do not realize that currently in the United States, an estimated *40 percent of all children* will live with their single mother (never married or divorced) and her boyfriend at

[In cohabitating relationships] young children are more likely to be injured or killed by their mother's live-in boyfriend than in biological families. Girls, for their part, are at higher risk of being sexually abused.[15]

some point before their sixteenth birthday.[16] With this in mind, shouldn't we consider *their* thoughts and feelings on the issue?

Truth be told, there's not a kid on this planet who wouldn't want his biological mom and dad committed to one another for life in a marriage relationship that provides a healthy, loving, stable family environment, free from abuse, strife, and the fear of separation. Why would we *intentionally* rob our kids of this?

Points to Ponder

1. In your own words, why is it absurd for young people to insist on becoming sexually experienced now so that they can satisfy their mate in the future?

    ✳ _____

    _____

    _____

2. Have you ever shed tears during a sad movie at the theater? Have you ever tried to play it off by saying, "I just got some salt from the popcorn in my eyes; that's all"?

    ✳ _____

    _____

    _____

    _____

3. What would you say to a friend who says it's no big deal that she's sleeping with her boyfriend because she plans to marry him someday?

✳ _____

_____

_____

_____

4. In your opinion, is masturbation a good way to satisfy yourself before marriage? Why or why not?

✳ _____

_____

_____

_____

5. What are some of the drawbacks associated with cohabitation (unmarried couples living together)?

✳ _____

_____

_____

6. How would you describe your home life?

✳ _____

_____

_____

_____

Chapter Eight

How does my home life and environment affect my sexual appetite?

*N*ewborn babies are the perfect picture of innocence, aren't they? They enter the world with a totally clean slate, with no history of hurting anyone or anything. They are also born with absolutely no sense of self or a personal identity. A baby's eyes are focused for hours a day on his parents' faces and the colorful world around him, not on his own appearance or stature. As he grows, he develops an idea of who he is based almost totally on what he is told about himself and how his caregivers convey his value and worth. This provides parents the wonderful opportunity to write beautiful messages on the blank canvas of their children's hearts. Unfortunately, it also makes it possible for hard-hearted individuals to carve painful impressions, leaving their children feeling worthless and wounded at the core of their being.

It is my observation that kids adopt one of three general identities, depending on how they have been treated and spoken to early in life, which subsequently influences their tendency to pursue sexual activity early in life. Which one do you identify with?

1. "I am valuable."

Children who are shown continual affection and verbal affirmation, combined with healthy doses of discipline, develop a personal sense of value and worth. When their home environment is loving, safe, and free from parental strife, kids form a relatively healthy view of themselves.

2. "I am a burden."

When a child is born into a volatile home life that consists of ongoing arguing, cruel name-calling, flaring tempers, and unstable relationships, the child concludes that he or she is a burden (children have the uncanny ability to blame *all* of the problems that take place around them on themselves). If a child is physically, verbally, or sexually abused, the notion of being a burden is driven into the deepest recesses of his or her heart. As a result, the child will battle feelings of insecurity,

When [parental] monitoring is part of a warm, supportive [parent/child] relationship, the child is likely to become a confident, well-educated adult, avoiding drug use and risky sex."[1]

worthlessness, and inferiority throughout life unless his or her childhood wounds are identified and ministered to. Without intervention, it is also likely that the child will repeat the dysfunction of the childhood and inflict similar wounds on his or her kids someday.

3. "I am invisible."

Unlike the child made to feel like a burden due to his parents' negative attention, this child's wound is the result of *not enough* parental attention. Parental neglect can manifest in the form of unmet physical needs or abandonment by one or both parents, but is often due to factors as subtle as parents' career demands or preoccupied lifestyles.

Perhaps a child's parents are hardworking professionals, successful community leaders, or prominent pastors for that matter. Then again, he may have a single mom who has no choice but to work long hours, and cannot help the fact that she is frequently not home. Whatever the case, a lack of attention, quality time, discipline, and parental interaction convey the painful message to a child that he or she is nothing special and not worthy of parents' time or energy. This causes a child to feel depressed, worthless, and desperate for recognition, which, more often than not, drives the child to *unhealthy* sources of attention.

The absence of a father, especially early in a young person's life, is a strong factor associated with adolescent sexual activity.[2]

Identity Type Influences Sexual Behavior

It's been said that all males have a certain question regarding their manhood that demands an answer. Likewise, all females crave a response to a particular question about their own femininity and identity. This gender-specific question nags at our hearts from early childhood and continues throughout our lives, especially if we get a negative response or no response at all during our formidable years.

According to John and Stasi Eldredge, for boys, the question is: ***"Do I have what it takes to be a man?"*** For girls, the question is, ***"Am I lovely?"***[3]

When our family relationships and early life experiences convey a resounding *no* to our most vulnerable question, or if there is a lack of affirmation one way or the other, we do the one thing that comes natural—*we search for someone to give us the response we crave.*

A young person may turn to a violent local gang for acceptance and validation or a loving Sunday school teacher, depending on who reaches out to him first. His allegiance will lie with whomever answers yes to his heart's question, even if this affirmation comes from a deceptive, manipulative source.

If we're operating out of a broken identity, we are on a desperate hunt for validation, and premarital sex can be a very alluring outlet.

Why some young men seek affirmation through premarital sex:

I was in the grocery store check-out line the other day and two teenaged boys in line behind me were carrying on a conversation about sports. (Not surprising, right?) One of the boys abruptly changed the topic of their discussion to comment about a magazine cover on the shelf in front of him. Apparently he noticed the headlines—a prominent actress and sex symbol was pregnant. The young man commented to his friend, "Wow, that's a lucky guy who knocked her up!" His statement was heartbreaking, but not at all a surprise. Manhood is often erroneously defined by a man's ability to "conquer" a female, and the sexier she is, the greater the "score."

> *I made a covenant with my eyes not to look with lust at a young woman* (Job 31:1 NLT).

I never went into the boys' locker room in high school, but I heard my share of rumors that originated there. Guys would brag and swap stories about who they fooled around with and how far they managed to get. The bigger breasted the girl, and the more a young man was able to coax her into doing, the more *attaboys* he received from his peers. In such cases, every pat on the back and sigh of envy communicates one thing to a boy: *"Yes, **I do** have what it takes to be man!"*

A young man's ability to manipulate a girl into having sex hardly exemplifies biblical manhood, but with no knowledge of such truths, his conquests with females make him "feel like a man." Sex, then, becomes the outlet he relies on to bolster his own distorted sense of self-confidence.

Why some young women seek affirmation through premarital sex

I really take offense when girls refer to another girl as a *slut*. Not only is it a cruel and derogatory word, but I don't believe there are any young girls who are capable of being such a thing. Are there girls who are so desperate for attention that they will give their bodies to one boy after another in hopes of feeling loved? Yes. But I have yet to meet a teenaged girl who sleeps around simply for the purpose of sexual gratification. It's *always* about getting her question answered—*Am I lovely?*

A guy looking to take advantage of a girl sexually knows exactly what kind of female to target and just what to say to her. He's on the lookout for an attractive girl who feels worthless. He knows that by telling her she means the world to him ("You are lovely to me!"), she'll most likely surrender her body. When he scores with the girl, dumps her, and then brags about his victory to his school-mates, it only drives home what she has always believed: *"No, I am **not** lovely!"*

What About You?

Has your childhood been less than ideal? Perhaps you've survived your parents' painful divorce. Maybe you have never met one or both of your parents. Then again, your parents may be happily married and yet life experiences have left you feeling empty and undervalued.

No matter the case, allow me to play the part of a big sister for a moment and offer some important advice:

Don't have sex in an effort to feel better about yourself! Surrendering your body is *not* going to uplift your soul. Furthermore, a boyfriend or girlfriend does not have the ability to heal the hurt in your heart. The temporary high of physical passion always fades and we are left with the all too familiar feelings of emptiness and regret. I know this because I experienced it. Take it from me, you have to bring your nagging hurts and internal struggles to the One who actually has the ability to do something about it—*God*.

In a national survey, nearly one-third of 15- to 17-year-olds, especially boys, said they had experienced pressure to have sex.[6]

Self-Esteem Versus God-Esteem

You made all the delicate, inner parts of my body and knit me together in my mother's womb. Thank you for making me so wonderfully complex! Your workmanship is marvelous—You watched me as I was being formed in utter seclusion, as I was woven together in the dark of the womb. You saw me before I was born. Every day of my life was recorded in your book. Every moment was laid out before a single day had passed. How precious are your thoughts about me, O God! They cannot be numbered! I can't even count them.... And when I wake up, you are still with me! (Psalm 139:13,15-18 NLT)

Your parents may or may not have planned to get pregnant with you, but that doesn't matter. The fact that you exist means *the God of the universe planned for you!* I don't know if you score a perfect ten for looks or if you're going through an awkward stage that consists of acne, bird legs, and braces, but I *do* know that we can't base our self-worth on such temporary, silly things.

That beating heart in your chest and the circulating air in your lungs testify to the fact that you are the handiwork of God Himself, and therefore He determines your value! For this reason, we don't need *self*-esteem (I am valuable because *I* love me); we need *God*-esteem (I am valuable because *God* loves me)! It is God's acceptance of me that allows me to accept me—make sense?

What does God think about you? Does He even think about you? Does He care about your hurts and disappointments? Does He have a plan for your life? Is He willing and able to heal your internal wounds?

You probably know that I believe the answer is *yes,* but so what. What do *you* believe? I can shout, "You matter to God!" from my rooftop all day long, but until you truly believe that, I'm wasting my time (and annoying my neighbors!). Log on to an online Bible program or pick that Bible up off the bookshelf, and then dig through it, looking for all the nuggets of gold where God describes how much He loves you. It's amazing how God can take a Scripture written for all people for all time and cause it to jump off the page as if to say, "I wrote this just for you!" Never experienced that? Well, ask the Holy Spirit to reveal God's Word to you and then—well, read it!

MAKE SURE YOU GET A VERSION OF THE BIBLE
that's easy for you to read—all the "thuses" and "thous" of the
King James Version can leave a person feeling like, "HUH?"

In addition to His Word, God may use loving and wise people in our lives to help heal our hearts, but He is the ultimate source of our transformation. I double-dog dare you to get alone in a quiet place and confide in God about all that is bothering and hurting you. You may not even understand completely why you are hurting, but if you take your emotions and needs to God in prayer, He will start working in those areas to bring about understanding and change. I know this from personal experience, and I long for you to know this from *your own* personal experience as well!

How will God answer your prayer? Well, that's for the God of the universe to decide—all I know is He *will* answer in His timing and in His way.

More About How Your Environment Affects Your Sexual Appetite

Be careful! Watch out for [attacks from] *your great enemy, the devil. He prowls around like a roaring lion, looking for* [some victim] *to devour* (1 Peter 5:8 NLT).

Did you know you have a spiritual enemy? Satan is not just a fable. He and his demonic soldiers are real, and they work day and night to take humanity captive. One of the ways the enemy tries to destroy you and me is by exploiting our sexuality, and he wants to accomplish this as early in our lives as possible. For this reason, the moral atmosphere we choose to surround ourselves with is *extremely* important. Consider the following illustration.

The Trojan Horse

If you've studied Greek mythology in school, you most likely recall the infamous Trojan horse in Virgil's Latin epic poem, *The Aeneid*. According to the tale, the Greeks wanted to bring about the demise of the city of Troy so they developed an ingenious covert operation. The Greeks pretended to sail away, leaving one man behind to present Troy with an enormous wooden horse. (Knowing my luck, I'd be the one sap picked out of the whole bunch to accomplish that daunting task!) The man told the Trojans that the horse was an offering and that if they would receive it into their city, they would have the "good fortune" they needed in order to defeat the Greeks.

Ignoring the adamant warnings from their priest, the Trojans accepted the gift and brought the massive structure into their heavily fortified city. You probably recall what happened next—at nightfall, thousands of Greek warriors poured out of the wooden horse and slaughtered the unsuspecting Trojans.

While I do not believe in the fairytales of Greek mythology, I do believe the Trojan horse illustrates a powerful military strategy that our spiritual enemy knows all too well. Satan is an expert at trespassing into unsuspecting households and destroying families from within. He accomplishes this through highly esteemed, seemingly innocent household items—*our media outlets.*

> *But I* [Jesus] *say, anyone who even looks at a woman with lust in his eye has already committed adultery with her in his heart* (Matthew 5:28 NLT).

Adultery, casual sex, perversion, and nudity are all accessible with the simple click of a remote control. Add the Internet and magazines and you've really got a smorgasbord of unclothed flesh to choose from!

CHECK IT OUT:
According to the Coalition for
the Protection of Children and Family:[7]

* ✳ 75 percent of prime-time television in the 1999–2000 season included sexual content.

* ✳ Over 80 percent of TV shows popular with teens contain sexual content.

* ✳ Movies have an 87 percent likelihood of presenting sexual material.

* ✳ The average age of first Internet exposure to pornography is 11 years old.

* ✳ The largest consumer of Internet pornography is the 12 to 17 age group.

Perhaps you are wondering, *"What's the big deal about looking at that stuff—it's not like I'm going to go out and do it!"* Oh, bless your sweet heart and naive mind! We can't feast our eyes on sexually stimulating images without provoking lust in our hearts, and once our hearts are consumed with lust, we become desperate to go out and gratify our sexual longings. As a result, it's most likely just a matter of time until we are compromising our standards and doing things we never thought we would do.

Pleasurable hormones, emotions, and physical sensations are all aroused when we behold sexually explicit images, and such feelings are addicting. Keep in mind, there's always a huge "crash" that follows. Once we are done looking at sexually stimulating images, we are bombarded with overwhelming feelings of disappointment and dissatisfaction, which only drives us to take another peek at graphic material in order to boost our mood. What a horrible cycle!

Are You Loyal to Your B.F.F.?

Carefully read the following scenario and imagine yourself and your best friend in this predicament:

There's a clique of guys and gals at school who are attractive and really fun. Even better, they totally dig you and want you to hang out with them. The challenge is that they can't stand your best friend in the whole wide world, even though he has never done anything to warrant their hatred. They rag on him all the time, make fun of him

"Adolescents who watch television with high levels of sexual content are twice as likely to initiate sexual intercourse and also more likely to initiate other sexual activities."[8]

and his family, and criticize pretty much everything that he values and stands for.

One Friday night, this outgoing clique of jocks and beauties invites you to go to the mall with them, and despite that "don't-do-it" feeling tugging at your heart, you accept their invitation. You feel like a million bucks when they pick you up in a tricked-out convertible and drive to the mall with the top down. As you walk around the mall, it feels like every young person is staring at you and the rest of the group with envy, and even though you'd never admit it, it's a cool feeling.

You're enjoying this "high" of sorts, when all of a sudden you spot your best friend walking in your direction! The clique spots him as well, and starts in with their insults and mockery. Your best friend is obviously trying to ignore their comments and just walk on by, when suddenly he spots you right in the middle of the group! He can't believe you're hanging with them!

How do you feel?

What do you say?

Let's Tie This Story in With the Theme of the Chapter

Check this Scripture out:

"Teens with high levels of exposure to rap videos, which often promote drug use, violence, and sex, are significantly more likely to acquire an STD."[9]

You adulterers! Don't you realize that friendship with the world makes you an enemy of God? I say it again: If your aim is to enjoy this world, you can't be a friend of God (James 4:4 NLT).

Let me break this passage down so that it's plain and clear. Humanity, as a whole, does not love God—or even like Him, for that matter. They insult Him, mock Him, reject what He stands for (as explained in the Bible), and even use his name as a curse word to express anger and disgust. So, when we "hang out" with worldliness, which includes watching perverted movies, logging onto sexually based Web sites, looking at "nudie" magazines, and partying in smoky drunken atmospheres with people who have no respect for God, we have joined ourselves in fellowship with those who make themselves enemies of God. In doing so, we have forsaken our covenant commitment to God, which is why the passage calls it adultery (adultery = disloyalty to one's marriage/covenant partner). We have rejected God's friendship and grieved the Holy Spirit. Yikes!

We are to be loving and friendly to those who don't know Christ, but we are not to entertain ourselves with their sinful habits, media, and objects. Do you want friendship with the world or friendship with the God of the Bible? Every one of us has to make that life-altering decision **and choosing *both* is not an option.**

What If My Parents Allow That Stuff in Our Home?

Ideally, your parents are doing their best to protect your eyes and ears from sexually stimulating media. If this is not the case, however, you're going to have to take a respectful yet radical stand in your home. If something inappropriate is on display, get up and leave the room.

> *"But among you there must not be even a hint of sexual immorality, or of any kind of impurity—because these are improper for God's holy people"* (Ephesians 5:3).

Let's define inappropriate, shall we? Obviously, nudity and sexual acts are not something we should gaze upon, but neither is coarse jesting or perverted language. Suggestive talk and sexual innuendoes are not appropriate for Christians, either, nor are they beneficial. Check out the scripture highlighted above.

By the way, just because we're 13 years old or older does not mean we have any business watching PG-13 movies. It's amazing what those film rating folks think is acceptable for a 13-year-old to watch—or adults for that matter! As a general rule, rated R films are not good to see, and most PG-13 aren't, either. Now, I didn't say they aren't *entertaining* to see! I mean that they are not good for the soul.

"Unfortunately, many teenagers get much of their 'sex education' from the media, which present a distorted view of sexual activity, associating it with fun, excitement, competition, danger, or violence, and rarely showing the risks of unprotected sex."[10]

In Summary

You are precious and worth protecting. Don't give the enemy access to the eye-gate or ear-gate of your soul. And don't use premarital sex to compensate for any negative feelings you have about yourself. Instead, turn to God and let Him heal you. Trade in self-esteem for God-esteem. Last but not least, while out renting movies, pass up the "nudie" flicks and check out the family picks!

Points to Ponder

1. Which of the three identities mentioned at the beginning of the chapter do you tend to indentify with, and why?

✳ _____

_____

_____

2. In your own words, explain the difference between seeking to have God-esteem versus self-esteem.

✳ _____

_____

_____

3. Are you aware of what you say when you sneeze? It sounds to me like most people clearly say, "hot shoes!" while sneezing. Odd, isn't it?

✳ _____

_____

_____

4. Why might a girl be vulnerable to being physically "used" by a guy? Why might a guy brag about his sexual experiences with a girl?

✳ _____

_____

_____

5. Are you honoring God and protecting your sexual appetite with your media selections? If not, what might you need to do differently?

✳ _____

_____

_____

6. In light of this chapter's "best-friend scenario," are you being a loyal covenant partner to God? If not, what are some ways you can change that?

✳ _____

_____

_____

Chapter Nine

How do I find a mate who's right for me?

I may have never met you, but I can confidently say I know something about you. *You have a tendency to rely on yourself instead of God.* There's no need to marvel at my astute observation, nor get defensive—it's true of every person. Like a toddler who insists on shouting "No Daddy, I can do it myself!" it is our human nature to assert our independence, as if to somehow prove to our Creator that we have everything under control (yeah, right). Oh sure, we eventually cry out to God for His help, but it is usually after we find ourselves utterly overwhelmed and helpless to cope with a dire circumstance of some sort.

The call to Christianity is *not* one of self-reliance and personal empowerment (despite what some trendy preachers proclaim these days). Biblical Christianity is about dependence on God's Spirit to save us, guide us, help us, and give us the grace we need to live each day for Him. It is about esteeming God's will for our lives over our personal agenda and surrendering to His competent leadership.

So how do we go about finding the right mate? The same way we should make every other significant life decision—*we rely on the Holy Spirit's guidance.*

Consider the essential life truths contained in these Scriptures—*"Trust in the Lord with all your heart and lean not on your own understanding. In all your ways acknowledge him and he shall direct your paths,"* (Prov. 3:6-7 NJKV). Let's look at how this passage applies to our desire to find the right mate:

Trust in the Lord with all your heart:

You can trust God with your future, including who you will marry. You can count on God to bring the right person at the right time into your life for the purpose of marriage. Is God forgetful? Uninterested? Irresponsible? Not at all! While He can be unpredictable, He is faithful, and we can confidently put our trust in Him.

Lean not on your own understanding:

Ever noticed that people tend to be on their best behavior while on a date? In dating relationships, guys don't usually lose their tempers, pass gas, or admit to having an addiction to pornography. Girls rarely nag, cry at the drop of a hat, or confess their true motives—"I'm looking for a wealthy man who will marry me and buy me everything I want."

The point is, we need the Holy Spirit to help us discern whether someone is or isn't the right mate for us as opposed to relying exclusively on our own impressions and feelings, which can be seriously misleading. Only God knows the true intent and condition of another person's heart, and we need to be sensitive to what He is telling us about someone we're interested in. God also speaks through people, so we should not ignore any "red flags" or concerns our friends or loved ones have about the person we're considering marrying.

In all of your ways acknowledge Him:

As previously discussed, we have a tendency to be self-reliant and call on God only when we are suffering. It's amazing to think that the God of the universe is ready and willing to guide us in every situation, but we forgo His help, preferring to face life in our own extremely limited strength and understanding. When it comes to finding a mate, we should include God in *every* aspect of the process—how we handle our feelings of attraction, who we enter into dating relationships with, how to prepare for marriage, and so on. We include Him by following the wisdom of His Word and asking Him to show us His will in all things. Our next point tells us what we can expect when we do this.

He shall direct your paths:

When we trust God, depend on Him more than our own limited understanding, and acknowledge Him in our desire to find a mate, He promises to direct our paths. Think about this—He not only directs *us* (see Prov. 3:6), but He directs *our paths*, which is to say, He dictates what comes our way.

You and I cannot possibly control who will and won't cross our paths tomorrow, but God can! He can ensure that we meet the person who is to be our soulmate for life. That sounds like a much better proposition to me than going from one singles event to the next, exhausting myself looking for Mr. Right! I'd much rather rest in knowing that as I serve God and pattern my life after the truths in His Word, He will make sure my future spouse and I find one another and recognize the need to be together.

Furthermore, we don't have to stress about figuring out who "the one" is. God does not hide His will from us so that we must anxiously search for clues as if we're solving some sort of Blue's Clues mystery. His will simply unfolds as we serve Him daily and live in obedience (notice I *didn't* say His

"Divorce is most likely to occur within the first five years."[2]

will simply unfolds as we live in continual rebellion to God and do whatever we want, whether godly or ungodly).

God's Way or the World's Way?

If we're going to find a mate God's way, we can't pattern our premarital standards and behaviors based on what we see our society doing. After all, the masses place very little trust in God (if any), tend to rely solely on their own understanding, and rarely acknowledge God in *any* area of their lives, and therefore, do not walk on God-ordained paths.

If, as young adults, we're cultivating dating relationships with the opposite sex while maintaining healthy boundaries, and all the while honoring God in every aspect of our relationships, there's nothing overtly wrong with that. There are some young people, however, who choose to forgo the traditional dating scene, preferring not to get involved as "more than friends" with members of the opposite sex while they prepare to meet the one whom God has set apart to be their mate. They choose to trust by faith that God will bring their future spouse across their path at the right time, and He will clearly reveal who that person is.

"Second marriages end in divorce more often than first marriages, with each divorce stressful on both adults and children."[3]

Is there any biblical precedence for this approach? Let's take a look.

An Old but True Story

Times have changed since the Bible days, but God's principles are still the same. Allow me to paraphrase the story of how God brought Isaac a wife, and then we'll discuss how the story applies to your desire to find the right mate. I encourage you to read the biblical account for yourself in Genesis 24.

Abraham was getting very old and was concerned that his son Isaac needed a wife. While sipping on a low-fat Starbucks frappuccino one morning (okay, a slight modification), Abraham began worrying that Isaac would marry a local woman who did not worship God. So Abraham called on his trustworthy servant to travel to the town where they previously lived to find the ideal wife for Isaac, since the women living there served God. Abraham's servant recognized that this was a very important task and he asked Abraham, "What if the young woman I find will not move here from your old hometown? Should Isaac move there to be with her?"

"No!" Abraham insisted. "We are living where God told us to, and my son cannot disobey God in order to get married. We must stay in God's will by staying here." Abraham went on to tell his servant, "If you find the right woman for Isaac, but she is not willing to come back here with you to live with us, then just come home without her—I won't blame you."

But the servant was worried, "What if I can't figure out which woman to choose?" Abraham explained that an angel would go to the city before him and give him a sign so he would know which woman was the right one for Isaac. So the servant vowed to do as Abraham asked and loaded up several camels for the journey. He packed gifts to give the special woman and her family once he found her, which included an insulated Starbucks travel mug (you never know!).

He traveled to Abraham's hometown and arrived one evening, just as the women were heading down to the well to draw water. The servant humbly prayed, "Oh Lord, give me success and show kindness to Abraham by showing me which woman to choose for Isaac. This is my request—I will ask one of them for a drink, and if she says yes, and offers water for my camels too, I will know she is the one! Thank you for your kindness, Lord" (see Gen. 24:12-14).

As he was still praying, a young woman named Rebekah arrived with a water jug on her shoulder. She was a beautiful lady who was saving herself for her husband and had never been intimate with a man. The servant spotted her, ran over to her, and asked, "May I have a drink?"

"The chief reasons for the prevalence of STDs among teenagers are early sexual activity, which increases the likelihood of having multiple high-risk partners,... and for women, the tendency to have sex with older partners."[4]

"Certainly, sir!" Rebekah kindly said, and gave him a grande caramel latte with a double shot of espresso. (Okay, she gave him some water.) She then offered to provide water for his camels, which appeared to be an answer to the servant's prayers! As she generously provided water for his camels, the servant watched her and prayed, "Lord, is this really the one?" He soon felt convinced that Rebekah *was* the one, so he gave her all kinds of costly jewelry and gifts and asked to meet her parents. He was so grateful that the Lord had answered his prayer, and when Rebekah agreed to take him to meet her parents, he fell to his knees and thanked the Lord!

Rebekah's family was very nice. The servant explained why he was there and that he hoped to bring Rebekah home to meet and marry Isaac. Rebekah's parents realized it was God's will that she leave their home and get married, but they were hesitant to see her go. They were sad that their daughter was leaving, but Rebekah assured them she was ready. The servant gave gifts to her parents (they absolutely loved the Starbucks mug!) and then left with Rebekah to take her to meet Isaac and his coffee-drinking family.

Meanwhile, Isaac was taking a walk in a field and prayerfully thinking about things. Suddenly, he looked up and saw the camels coming. When Rebekah saw Isaac, she noticed him from far off and wanted to know who he was. The servant explained that he was Isaac, the man she was to marry. Isaac and Rebekah met and married, and Isaac loved his wife very much! She was a special comfort to him after his mother died.

Isaac and Rebekah went on to have children together, and their children had children, and so on and so on, until finally Jesus Christ was born through their descendants!

Now please don't panic and think I'm about to suggest that you have an arranged marriage! (Can you imagine who your parents would pick for you?) I simply want to highlight some of the spiritual principles evident in this historical account.

✳ Abraham was concerned that his son Isaac needed a wife.

In this story, we can view Abraham as a type (representation) of God the Father. Just as Abraham was aware that it was time for Isaac to get married, God also knows when we are ready for marriage. He *is* concerned with when and whom we marry.

✳ Abraham was worried that Isaac would marry a woman who did not worship God.

We are commanded in Scripture not to marry an unbeliever (see 2 Cor. 6:14). It is very difficult to serve God when our mate objects to our faith, or simply chooses not to serve God alongside us. And how confusing it is for kids to have parents who don't agree on who God is!

✳ **Abraham called on his trustworthy servant to find the ideal wife for Isaac.**

The servant can be viewed as a type (representation) of the Holy Spirit, who is at work in the earth today. When God the Father decides it's time for us to get married, the Holy Spirit leads us to that person. For this reason, we don't have to stress about finding a mate.

✳ **Abraham was clear that his son could not disobey God in order to get married.**

If we know that God has called us to live in a certain place, serve in a specific ministry, or fulfill a particular assignment, we shouldn't neglect that to get married. For example, if a man is called to the mission field but a woman asks him to give up mission work to marry her, she's not the right one for him. Certainly our assignments from God change over the years, and the missionary may eventually be called to stay home, but this must be according to God's plan, not an attempt to satisfy someone else's plan for him.

✳ **If you find the right woman for Isaac, but she is not willing, come home without her.**

Even if it's God's will that two people be joined together in marriage, He does not force this on them. Marriage is always the result of each person's freewill decision. Sometimes a person will feel confident he has found the one he is to marry, but the one he has set his sights on does not reciprocate such feelings. In such cases, we would never want to insist that someone marry us based on what "God showed us." The person God has for us will *want* to be with us as much as we want to be with him or her.

✳ *The servant would know which woman was the right one for Isaac.*

The Holy Spirit knows which person is right for us. As previously stated, we can trust God to bring a suitable mate into our lives. We don't have to exhaust ourselves trying to make something happen at the wrong time or with the wrong person.

✳ *Rebekah was a beautiful lady who was saving herself for her husband and had never been intimate with a man.*

There are two things to point out here. First, it's no coincidence that the servant/Holy Spirit noticed the one who was saving herself for her husband. This gesture of faith and obedience to God gets His attention! Also, beauty and premarital virginity are always linked together in the Bible. A woman of virtue has an attraction that supersedes physical beauty.

✳ *The helper asked to meet Rebekah's parents.*

The Holy Spirit will often give parents peace or a sense of concern about someone their kids are dating or considering marrying. We do a great disservice to ourselves if we ignore any concerns our parents may have about a potential spouse since God often leads us through our parents' (or guardians') discernment.

✳ *Rebekah assured her parents she was ready [to get married].*

Don't let anyone pressure you into getting married—your parents, church leaders, friends, or your fiancé! Simply stated, if you lack peace about getting married, don't go through with it. Even if the wedding invitations have gone out, it's not too late to change your mind. It is too late to back out of the relationship, however, once you are married.

✳ *Isaac was taking a walk in a field and prayerfully thinking about things.*

Notice what Isaac *wasn't* doing while he waited on the servant to bring him a wife. First, he wasn't making out with another girl. Second, he wasn't pacing back and forth worried that God would somehow drop the ball and fail to bring him a suitable wife. He was at peace, trusting that the servant/Holy Spirit would bring his wife to him according to His own perfect plan. We should do the same.

Teenage fathers tend to have limited financial resources, poor academic performance, and high dropout rates."[6]

✳ When Rebekah saw Isaac, she noticed him and wanted to know who he was.

Young people often express their concern, "What if I'm not attracted to the person God picks to be my spouse?" My traditional reply—"Then God isn't very bright, is He?" Of course God knows attraction is a necessary part of a marriage relationship, and certainly in His all-knowing nature, He is plenty wise enough to pick a mate for us that we will find attractive. I don't care how godly someone is or how well you two get along; if you aren't physically attracted to him or her, don't get married!

✳ Isaac and Rebekah went on to have children together, and their children had children, and so on and so on until finally Jesus Christ was born through their descendants!

Our union with our spouse is always about the bigger picture—God's purpose in the earth. While we do enjoy companionship and intimacy with our spouse, God is working to accomplish something more significant than our own fulfillment. As we rear godly offspring, serve God alongside each other, and determine to help our mates accomplish all that God is calling them to do, our relationship becomes *eternally* significant. As a result, we can leave a legacy that influences our family and others for generations to come!

WHAT IF YOU HAD TO PICK *ONE* FRIEND
and that was the *only* friend you could spend time with for the
rest of your life? You couldn't hang out with any other friends.
What factors would be important in choosing that friend? Similarly,
when we choose a mate, we are picking the *one and only* member
of the opposite sex that we will spend the rest of our lives with!
He or she will be our date for every movie night, banquet,
wedding, vacation, and event that we attend for the duration
of our lives—not to mention our permanent roommate. Given
that reality, what attributes do you feel are important to consider
and which ones are not so important when choosing a mate?

How Will I Know When I've Found My Future Spouse?

Modern pregnancy tests make it easy for women to get an answer to the question, "Am I pregnant?" Two lines—*yes*. One line—*no*. That's virtually all there is to it. If only there were a test that provided a concrete yes or no to the question, "Should I marry this person?" While there is no such litmus test, there actually is a way to know with confidence whether we should marry someone. *We can hear from God.*

We don't hear from God the same way we hear from people, with our physical ears. We listen to the voice of God with our spiritual ears. That's why Jesus continually said, *"Let him who has ears to hear, hear what the Spirit is saying."*

(See Matthew 11:15; 13:9,43; Mark 4:9,23; 7:16; Luke 8:8; 14:35.)

Did you know you have spiritual ears? The Lord is continually speaking to us by His Spirit, but we don't always recognize His voice. To learn more about how to hear God, I recommend Peter Lord's book, appropriately named *Hearing God*.[7] It is a tremendous resource and training tool for developing our spiritual sense of hearing.

In addition to speaking to us by His Spirit, God also reveals His will to us through His Word, through confirming circumstances, and through people (godly counsel). If all of these avenues are pointing to a yes, we can trust we have entered into God's will and proceed with marriage without fear of having missed the mark.

How can we choose the right mate? *Ask God for direction and obey what He tells us.* Consider the offer God extends to us in James 1:5—if we lack wisdom, we can ask God what we should do, and He will not frown on our uncertainty, but will instead gladly answer us.

Do you know you can ask God questions and bring inquiries to God in prayer? Do you realize God has promised to answer your questions and show you what to do?

Learning to discern God's will has lifetime benefits that go beyond choosing the right mate. The Christian life is meant to be lived with a daily assurance that we are smack-dab in the middle of God's perfect will for our lives; this brings the confidence and peace of mind we need in order to endure trying and difficult seasons.

Don't Make This Mistake

Our desire to find our future mate is accompanied by our everyday interactions with members of the opposite sex. At times, we will form attractions toward a certain someone and perhaps wonder if there's any potential for a "love match." It is at this point that some Christians make a serious mistake. We know our future mate needs to be a Christian, so we simply ask the person we're interested in, "Are you a Christian?"

"Why yes, I am!" they quickly respond. We take this profession of Christianity at face value and make premature assumptions about his or her spirituality. It's as if we simply check the "Christian box" on our list of marital prerequisites with hardly any objectivity.

Anyone can *say* he or she is a Christian. As a matter of fact, nationwide polls indicate that over 80 percent of Americans profess to be Christians. Why do we teach evolution instead of intelligent design in our public schools if the large majority of our country identifies with the God of the Bible? The answer is simple—there are lots of people naming the name of Christ who, in actuality, do not know or serve Him. They may own a Bible and even attend church, but like my husband always says, "Sitting in church doesn't make you a Christian any more than sitting in McDonald's makes you a Happy Meal!"

We can't know if someone is a Christian until we have time to observe the way that person lives his or her life. It's not that we arrogantly evaluate an individual's Christian performance; instead we look for evidence that points to a sincere versus shallow commitment to Christ. What a tragedy it is to marry someone under the impression he (or she) is a Christian, only to find that person is not committed to prayer, biblical standards, Spirit-led living, or Christ-like love.

Don't Make These Mistakes, Either

Here are some additional mistakes singles often make:

To reiterate a point previously made, we often ignore our parents' and friends' warnings and honest concerns about our dating relationships. If the people who love us have a "bad feeling" about someone we're involved with, we should take their reservations to heart and give careful consideration to the validity of their concerns, instead of merely defending the relationship. Too often, young people marry someone despite their loved ones' warnings, only to find that their family and friends were right about the person all along.

The following factors may play a part in an adolescent's decision to become sexually active: early entrance into puberty, poverty, poor school performance, lack of academic and career goals, a history of sexual abuse or parental neglect, and cultural or family patterns of early sexual experience.[8]

Don't misinterpret strong emotions as the Holy Spirit's leading. Even in the midst of the goose bumps, hot flashes, sweaty palms, and butterflies that accompany feelings of attraction and adoration, the Holy Spirit may be shouting, "No, she's not the one!" We need to be careful to discern the difference between our emotions and what God is truly telling us.

Beware of bogus signs from God. Young people often assume ironic or "mystical" experiences are an indication that God has ordained a certain relationship, when in reality, this is not the case. For example, a girl once told me, "I know I'm supposed to marry this guy because the first time he called me on the phone, the song, 'You're the One' came on the radio!" A young man shared with me, "I know my girlfriend is my soul mate for life because her middle name is the same as my mother's, and my mom passed away when I was two." That girl very well may be his soul mate for life but it's not because she shares his mother's name. Remember, we're to be led by the Spirit of God, not coincidence or unrelated signs.

Out of desperation, many people marry the first person who takes an interest in them even though the relationship is somewhat lacking in chemistry and companionship. Out of fear they may never meet or attract someone they really respect, they settle for a mediocre relationship. Not a good idea!

Don't overlook someone's extreme shortcomings just because you are anxious to be married. Marriage is far too serious a commitment to make as a result of impatience.

Take an objective look at the person you're with, and don't be in denial about his or her flawed character just because you don't like the idea of waiting on someone more suitable to come along. Better to marry the right person a few years later than the wrong person right away.

Whatever you do, don't assume someone is going to change just because you two get married! As a matter of fact, in marriage, people tend to become *more* of what they already are. If she's insecure now, she'll be even more insecure after marriage. If he loses his temper now, he'll be even more temperamental after saying *I do.* Yes, God can change people, but we can never afford to marry someone with the hope that they will change, because they often don't. When considering marrying someone, ask yourself, "If this person didn't change one bit, could I live with that?" If the answer is no, don't get married. It's a huge mistake! And in the long run, it's much easier to remain single and find a more compatible person than to try to change someone after marriage.

Unrealistic Expectations

I cannot close this chapter without stressing one final imperative point. *Just because we maintain our virginity and marry the one God has for us does not mean our marriage will be utter bliss all the time!* By its very nature, marriage is challenging. The reason we honor God with our love life (wait until we're married to have sex and marry the one He has for us) is ultimately because we love *Him!* The marital companionship we reap is the icing on the cake. Furthermore, the marital obstacles we encounter become divine opportunities to mature in persevering love.

Now that we've discussed issues surrounding finding a mate, let's look at how to go about picking up the pieces if we've already lost our virginity or sexual innocence through premature sexual experiences.

Points to Ponder

1. Do you tend to trust God with your life or try to control things in your own strength?

✳ _____

_____

_____

2. Proverbs 3:7 tell us we should acknowledge God in all of our ways. Give some examples of how we can practically go about this.

✳ _____

_____

_____

3. In your opinion, why is it important to be able to hear the Lord's voice with our "spiritual" ears?

✳ _____

_____

_____

4. Look back over the list of mistakes singles often make when it comes to selecting a spouse. Which one stands out the most to you and why?

✳ _____

_____

_____

5. Why is it that we usually yawn when we see other people yawn?

✳ _____

_____

_____

6. What are three characteristics you *do not* want your future mate to have?

✳ _____

_____

_____

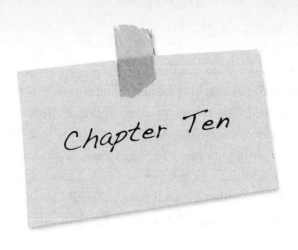

Chapter Ten

What if I've already had sex?

I was sitting in the third row at a Christian singles conference thinking to myself, "This lady is totally old but still looks really pretty!" The conference speaker was only in her 40s, but you know how it is—when we're young, everyone over 29 seems feeble and elderly. The vibrant lady was addressing the issue of abstinence and managed to stir the whole stadium into a frenzy by posing one question: *"Isn't it great to be a virgin?"*

While everyone around me was whooping, hollering, and doing some sort of "raise the roof" motion with their hands, I sat there motionless, overwhelmed by the reality of my response to the question.

I don't know if it's great to be a virgin because I'm not one.

Maybe you've been reading this book and all the while feeling like I did at that conference—like you've blown it and it's too late to do anything about it. While it's true that we can't undo the decisions of our past, it is also true that we can choose a different course for our future. That being said, if you've already had sex but would like a second chance to honor God with a life of sexual purity, I've got good news— you can have that second chance starting right now!

I want to walk you through the five steps to what I call the transformation process, but first, I have to ask you one thing—did you read the previous chapters? If you turned right to this section without reading the preceding material, that doesn't mean you're a dork or anything. It just means that there are going to be statements in the upcoming text that aren't going to have as much clarity or meaning for you as I would like them to have. With this in mind, please go ahead and start with the first chapter and patiently read your way through to this point. Don't worry, I too know what it's like to pray, "Dear Lord, give me patience...and give it to me right now!"

The Transformation Process

STEP ONE: *Repentance*

The healing process always starts with admitting how we have failed and repenting to God. It's important to note that repentance is more than saying we're sorry; it's an act of turning our backs on a certain behavior and determining never to do it again. When we repent for premarital sexual activity, we aren't just asking God to forgive our actions from the past; we are also asking Him to help us never repeat those actions in the future!

> *If we confess our sins, He* [God] *is faithful and just to forgive us our sins and to cleanse us from all unrighteousness* (1 John 1:9 NKJV).

It sure would be nice if, upon repenting, an invoice dropped down from Heaven that said, *"Your sins are officially forgiven; signed, God."* Instead, we must receive forgiveness by faith, trusting that God has released us from guilt based on His Word and Christ's sacrifice. It is only after we have repented for our sexual sins and received God's forgiveness by faith that we are ready for the next step in the transformation process.

STEP TWO: *Realize and Release*

Throughout my book *Choosing to Wait: A Guide to Inspiring Abstinence*, I help parents understand what a key role they play in the development of their kids' outlook on premarital sex. I go into great detail about how we, as parents, should inspire and empower our kids to value and protect their virginity, and the book is full of practical ways parents can go about this. I said that to say that while I do believe you are responsible for your decisions, it is important to realize that a lack of parental support may have paved the way for the sexual pitfalls you've encountered.

God desires that parents *"train up their children in the way they should go"* (see Prov. 22:6), meaning they are to instruct and motivate their kids based on biblical truths. When parents fail to do this (for whatever reason), their kids are more vulnerable and likely to fall into life's many snares and traps. The reason it's important to acknowledge that our parents may have neglected to properly prepare us to overcome sexual temptation is because it's an essential part of freeing ourselves from *false guilt*. Allow me to illustrate this point with a testimony from a young lady I met in college who prefers to remain anonymous:

> *I was raised in a home with a single mother and had no relationship with my father. My mother worked long hours to provide for my brother and me, which meant in middle school, I had several unsupervised hours every day after school. In the eighth grade, I started spending more and more time with my boyfriend, who traditionally came over to my house every afternoon before my mom came home from work. Having constant alone time with my boyfriend led to fooling around and eventually to having sex; I became sexually active at just 13 years of age.*
>
> *As I got older, I realized I should not*

have had premarital sex, and I repented to God and chose abstinence for the remainder of my single years. However, I battled constant feelings of guilt and shame as a host of tormenting thoughts often bombarded my mind—"You are cheap and worthless! You are not a treasure; you are easy trash! You are used goods!"

I eventually got victory over those kinds of thoughts and feelings and no longer carried that guilt and shame, but one aspect was essential to my emotional healing. At one point, I realized that while I chose to have sex (something I acknowledged through repentance), I was also placed in a vulnerable position that I was ill-equipped to handle. Furthermore, my mother did not teach me about the sacredness of sex, and she was not nearly protective enough or tuned-in during my adolescent years. I realized that I, as a young girl, was not an "easy piece of trash," but rather, a naive girl whose lack of parental involvement set me up for failure.

After properly identifying how my parents failed to warn, instruct, and protect me from premature sexual activity, I went to God in prayer and forgave them. My mother did the best she could based on how her parents raised her, and the fact that she had to be the single breadwinner for our family made it especially difficult for her to supervise my activities. My father suffered from his own childhood traumas, and although there was no excuse for his decision to abandon my brother and me, I was able to have mercy toward him instead of bitterness—he really missed out by not getting to know us.

Just as this inspiring young lady's testimony illustrates, once we identify how our parents "dropped the ball," we are more apt to quit carrying around unnecessary guilt for circumstances that were beyond our control. In other words, we must repent for the part that *we* played in our sexual sin, but we should not beat ourselves up or take the blame for the part *others* played.

Next, we must release to God any resentment we have toward our parents and choose to forgive. Remember, forgiveness does not mean what someone did to us was okay; it just means we are willing to release their hurtful acts, the same way God releases us and forgives our sins.

We can never reach out and receive God's healing touch if our fists are clinched tight holding onto bitterness.

STEP THREE   Reconnect

It is most often the case that when young persons are sexually active, they are in disobedience to their parents—whether through lying about where they have been and what they've been up to or simply by disobeying their parents

While both parents and teens report that they have talked to each other about sex and relationships, there appears to be a disconnect: twice as many parents as teens maintain that these conversations happen often (85 percent to 41 percent).[2]

by having sex, knowing that the parents would not approve.

When we are in rebellion and disobedience toward our parents, we usually isolate and distance ourselves from them—a defense mechanism to avoid getting exposed and caught.

During this step in the transformation process, we must reconnect with our parents (or caregivers) and authorities (youth ministers, mentors, etc.). After all, they're the people in this world who love us the most! If we're going to successfully overcome the temptation to compromise our sexuality in the future, we need the accountability, support, and care of our "home team."

Are there acts of deceit and rebellion that you need to repent for to your parents? Have you been lying to them about certain things that you need to come clean about? It's never pleasant to confess our sins to our parents, but it is so very refreshing to come out of guilt, fear, and hiding!

Do your part to rebuild a bridge of trust between you and your parents. (Sometimes writing a letter helps us best express ourselves.)

"Adolescence is often characterized as a time of waning adult influence, a period when young people distance themselves from the values and behaviors of their elders. There is some validity to this observation, but it need not be true, nor is such a disconnect necessarily a good sign."[3]

STEP FOUR: *Restoration*

When I was about eight years old, I used to love to go play at Julie's house, my best friend. One day in particular, we were running through the living room and Julie accidentally slammed into a coffee table, knocking one of her mother's vases to the floor. The loud crash immediately silenced our giggles. We stared wide-eyed at the broken pieces and wondered how in the world we were going to avoid serious punishment.

The solution was obvious—we had to glue that vase back together before Julie's mom saw it! We got out the super-glue and carefully patched the colorful vase back together. By the time the glue dried, we were quite relieved. You could only tell the vase had been repaired if you looked closely at it. We put it back on the coffee table, only now the vase was nestled behind an artificial plant to disguise the cracks. Our hope was that Julie's mom wouldn't pay close attention to her beloved vase. (Did I mention it was an heirloom?) Having saved the day with our "brilliant" restoration efforts, Julie and I went back to playing and forgot all about the ordeal. (I wonder if she ever got caught and disciplined for that?)

For many years, this was my understanding of God's restoration—He takes the broken pieces of my life (my hurts, sins, and mistakes) and patches them back together to make me look as if everything is fine. As long as I keep a safe distance from others and don't allow them to get too close, they won't notice how fragile and broken I really am.

I have since learned that God's restoration is not about disguising our brokenness, but rather, totally healing it. What if Julie and I could have taken that broken vase to the artist who created it? And what if that artist then took those broken pieces, melted, molded, and reset the shape of the vase, and then reapplied the decorative artwork by hand? When he was done, there would be no cracks or broken pieces, only a beautiful masterpiece that need not be disguised or hidden.

Restoration in our lives is not about covering up what we've done or masking the hurts we've acquired; it's about getting totally healed. Our experiences with premature sex may have left us feeling like "used goods" or undervalued. Then again, maybe we feel guilty for having been the initiator in the sexual relationship. No matter the case, we need to know that God, our loving Creator, wants to restore the way we see ourselves.

There is no magic formula for bringing about this restoration. It simply comes as a result of desiring to know God more and receiving His healing touch. The more we learn who God is, the more He shows us who we are, and equally important, who we are *not*. As we relate to God through reading His Word and enjoying open and honest discussions about Him and with Him, God will heal our wounds and redefine how we view ourselves. We don't need to cover up our shortcomings before entering into prayer. On the contrary, we should release our hurts, disappointments, and failures into His competent hands. In time, He will bring renewal.

STEP FIVE: *Renewal*

We know we've entered into renewal when we no longer identify with the hurt and guilt associated with the sins of our past. While we likely remember how the pain felt, we are no longer victims of that pain. In the renewal phase, it's not that we suddenly have it all together and can boast in our Christian performance—far from it! It's that we are more dependent than ever on the Holy Spirit to strengthen us to live the Christian life. Righteous living is a matter of will, but not willpower; the issue is *will* we surrender to the Spirit's leadership in our lives?

A natural byproduct of having passed through repentance, realization and release, reconnection and restoration into the renewal phase of the transformation process is that we are now in a position to take our past mess-ups and turn them into encouraging messages! By this point, we have learned so much through our experiences and grown so significantly in our faith that we have a testimony that can inspire and significantly impact our peers.

Virginity: More Than a Physical State

The last thing I want you thinking is that there's no point in abstaining from sex since you've already "blown it." As previously discussed, virginity is more than a physical state; it is a state of mind. It is a decision to wait until marriage to have sex based on the belief that there are spiritual implications to sex. While there is no way to reclaim our physical virginity once we have become sexually active, we can *always* make the decision to stop. *At any time* we can begin trusting God's plan and reserving our hearts and bodies for marriage.

Allow me to be the loving voice of reason in your life that reminds you, you *do* have a choice.

So, after all we've discussed up to this point, what is your choice? Are you going to remain abstinent until marriage? If your answer is yes (I really, really hope it is!), the next chapter is especially important.

1. In your opinion, what's the difference between being sorry we got caught versus being sorry for what we did?

*
_____
_____
_____

2. In what ways have your parents failed to prepare you to face and overcome sexual temptation? Are you willing to forgive them for that?

*
_____
_____
_____

3. Do you need to repent to your parents for anything? When and how might you go about doing this?

*
_____
_____
_____

4. Out of the five steps in the transformation process described in this chapter, which one do you identify with the most at this point in your life, and why?

✳ _____

_____

_____

5. What type of kid were you: the kind that would steal Easter eggs out of other kids' baskets or the kind that would give eggs to the kids who didn't have many?

✳ _____

_____

_____

6. Where do you stand on the issue of premarital abstinence at this point, and why?

✳ _____

_____

_____

Chapter Eleven

How in the world do I resist having sex until I'm married?

There's nothing worse than getting halfway through a recipe and then realizing you're missing a crucial ingredient. Or how about assembling something only to find that you're missing one key component you need in order to finish?

Along those lines, I don't want to see you make a commitment to premarital abstinence today and then lack the strength you need to follow through in the future.

There's no denying that struggles are going to come, because remaining sexually pure is no easy task. However, it is my desire that you have a realistic idea about what it takes to overcome those struggles so you can follow through with your commitment.

Let's talk about what to do when you first decide you want to pursue abstinence, and then we'll move on from there.

1. Announce and celebrate your decision.

Have you committed to be abstinent until marriage? Then blow up some balloons, order a cake, and bid on a disco ball and bellbottoms on eBay—it's time to celebrate! Okay, you don't have to throw a "groovy" abstinence-themed party, but I *do* encourage you to celebrate your decision one way or another. Furthermore, it's imperative that you share your resolution with your parents, friends, and loved ones. Keeping your commitment to abstinence a secret between you, God, and your diary doesn't provide enough accountably—you need to include others in this journey.

Back to the idea of celebrating. Here are some special ways you can commemorate your decision to wait for your mate:

* **Have a ring ceremony** where your parents place a "promise ring" on your wedding finger (various churches host such events). Write some vows concerning your commitment to abstinence and read them to your parents. Keep that ring on until your wedding day as a constant reminder of your commitment.

* **Invite friends and family over** to your house and explain the decision you have

made and why you made it. Enjoy a meal or some refreshments afterward.

✳ **Write a letter to your future spouse** explaining your commitment to wait for him or her. Have your family take a seat on the couch and read your letter to them. Frame the letter and put it on display somewhere where you will see it often. (Imagine giving that letter to your spouse someday as a wedding gift!)

Can you think of some other ideas? (If all else fails, you can host a groovy "I chose abstinence" party!) There are many ways to go about it, but I encourage you to do something that celebrates your decision and allows others to rejoice with you.

2. Hang around like-minded people.

If you want to keep your commitment to abstinence going strong, make friends with people whose lifestyles do not contradict your commitment. We don't have any business hanging around with sexually active singles or friends who entertain themselves with sexually graphic media. There's an old saying, "You are what you eat." Likewise, we become what we are surrounded by. Surround yourself with people who point you in the right direction, not people who pull you away from your goals.

And for Pete's sake, don't date someone who doesn't have your same commitment to sexual purity! That's like trying to run a marathon with a sumo wrestler riding on your back. (Feel free to pause a moment to reflect on that mental image.)

3. Be smart.

One day while sitting in a college algebra class, a guy sat down next to me and expressed how very nervous he was about taking the test that was soon to be distributed. He went on and on about how badly he wanted to pass, and how he desired to get a really good grade in the course. Ironically, when I asked him how long he studied for the test he said, "I didn't."

Throughout this book, we've gone over lots of principles and practices that will help you succeed in your quest to be abstinent. *Apply them.* (Wow, that was profound, wasn't it?) Don't expect to coast through your single years without compromising your commitment to abstinence unless you are willing to follow through with the various steps and strategies as depicted in this book (and other quality materials relating to abstinence).

They say elephants never forget a thing, but since you and I are not elephants, we have to

"Common risk factors for sexual activity among adolescents are living in a socioeconomically disadvantaged community, substance abuse, antisocial behavior, and association with deviant peers."[1]

review and remind ourselves of things from time to time. For this reason, you will want to read this book again in the future, along with any other books that help remind you why you chose abstinence in the first place. As previously stated, however, you must apply what you read if it's going to do any good.

4.　Be the real thing!

Lot's of kids are good at playing the game. They go to church, attend Christian concerts, and sport Christian T-shirts on a regular basis. They can recite a few key Scriptures from the Bible and they are the first ones to raise their hands if a volunteer is needed to pray over a meal.

Sadly, it is sometimes the case, however, that such young people are going through the motions of Christianity, but have yet to truly experience Christ in their lives. In other words, they have *religion* down pat, but lack a meaningful *relationship* with God, which makes for a very unfulfilling life.

Please don't settle for playing the game. If you're going to be a Christian, make sure that knowing Christ is at the center of your focus. Otherwise, you'll end up like I did—a teenager who talks a big talk but has no real strength of character to walk the walk.

As a freshman in high school, I thought premarital abstinence was just for nerds and "goody-two-shoes" types, but later in the school year, I heard a message at church that sex outside of marriage was wrong, no matter who we are. From that point on, I encouraged my peers to abstain from sex, but the truth was, I struggled to take my own advice. You can imagine how humiliating it was for me when I, the girl known for "preaching" abstinence to my friends, dropped out of college my sophomore year because I was pregnant!

What factors led to my crisis of belief—saying one thing but living something different?

One, I didn't understand *why* God didn't want me having sex before marriage; I only knew I wasn't supposed to. That is why I have taken the time to write this book and answer the question, "Why wait?" I want you to have the knowledge I lacked at your age so that you don't fall into the same traps I did!

Second, I understood Jesus as my Savior (Christ died for my sins on the cross), but I didn't revere Him as Lord (Christ deserves my obedience). Consequently, I was still living for myself and doing things my way, which contradicts the Bible's description of Christianity and never yields good results.

Savior – Lord = False; Savior + Lord = True

Somewhere in our country's spiritual history we falsely started separating Savior and Lord, as if we could accept Christ as our Savior but postpone

"At least one-third of teenage parents are themselves products of adolescent pregnancy."[2]

(or forgo) making Him the Master (Lord) of our lives. As a young person, I thought that because I had walked down to an altar and repeated a prayer for salvation as prompted by a minister, I was saved and would go to Heaven when I died. What I didn't realize at the time was that *salvation was not just about accepting Christ's sacrifice on my behalf, but about offering my life as a living sacrifice on His behalf!* In other words, He died for me so that I could live for Him, which meant doing things *His* way for a change.

Have you ever watched the music awards on TV? A girl will get out there and perform with her breasts falling out of her top and her booty shaking all over the stage while singing sexually graphic lyrics. Then, when she steps up to the podium to receive an award, she'll begin her speech by saying, "I'd like to thank Jesus Christ, my Savior, for blessing my life and bringing me to this point."

That is a prime example of how we can become deceived. She has no commitment to serving Christ, but still wants Him to bless and guide her life. What's more, she is so out of touch with God's nature that she actually thinks He could be pleased with the way she just behaved on stage. Tragically, she wrongly attributes her worldly "success" to God's blessing and approval.

My Story

As a teenager, when I first prayed the prayer to accept Christ, I wanted the assurance of going to Heaven, but I had no intention of surrendering my life over to God. After praying at the altar, I walked back to my sanctuary chair with a pamphlet in hand that assured me I was saved, but in my heart, I was as self-willed as I had always been. It wasn't until a series of hardships humbled me later in life that I came to the end of myself and made the decision to follow Christ.

I am confident I became born again in that moment—all alone in my bedroom with my Bible, tear-stained cheeks, and a heartfelt prayer—not when I went up to the altar and repeated a prayer years before. Emotions were involved in my born-again experience, but it was the drastic, permanent change in my inner desires and motives that showed me the transformation was more than emotional; *it was a miraculous spiritual conversion.*

It was after this experience that I met my husband, and I am happy to say that, by God's grace, we overcame sexual temptation. Having then realized many of the principles I've shared throughout this book, my husband and I did not have sex before we were married (which is a big deal because I'm *very* attracted to him!).

What Does Your Heart Tell You?

One of the ways we know we are truly saved is that we have a new desire to please God. Even though we still feel tempted to sin, there's something inside of us that doesn't want to give in. That "something" is the Holy Spirit—God's Spirit who comes to live in us when we accept Christ. The

Bible refers to Him as "the Helper" because His purpose is to help us live a godly life that we could not possibly live without His guidance. (Cool, huh?)

It sure will be hard for you to live a sexually pure life if you don't have the Holy Spirit to empower you. On the contrary, I have all the confidence in the world that with God's help, you can totally succeed at this! Having God as our source of strength makes all the difference. (If you aren't sure if you're saved, or if you want a better explanation of how to get saved, please go back and take a closer look at the quiz, "Am I a good person?")

To summarize, the key to your success in remaining abstinent until marriage is directly related to your relationship and dependency on God. If that sounds a bit simplistic to you, it's because it is! No matter what circumstance you face or what temptation life throws your way, you will overcome if you truly live with God as your Lord, Savior, and loving Father.

For those who prefer a more "down to earth" translation, let me say it like this—*if you and God are "tight," it's gonna be all right!*

Don't Be a Lone Ranger

It may appear "manly" when a cowboy rides off into the sunset all by himself in western movies, but in real life, there's nothing brave about isolating ourselves. Another key to your success in remaining abstinent involves your willingness to lean on others.

Sing with me! *"Lean on me...when you're not strong...and I'll be your friend...I'll help you carry on...for, it won't be long 'till I'm gonna need...somebody to lean on."*

It's an old song, but it has a very relevant message. There are going to be times when you need the accountability, advice, encouragement, prayer, and support of others. Go ahead and seek out and start investing in those kinds of strong friendships and relationships now so that when you are going through trying circumstances and need someone to lift you up, you will have people to go to.

Perhaps there are certain adults and peers at your school, church, extracurricular activities, or in your community who inspire you to live for God and achieve your goals. (Maybe you are blessed with parents who fit this description as well.) Those are the people you want to surround yourself with and confide in when you need help. These relationships, especially with wise and caring adults, can make *all the difference* when you are tempted to compromise your commitment to abstinence.

Pass It On

I can't believe in just a few short paragraphs, you'll be done with this book! It's time you start looking ahead. Now that you've read through this study, can you think of some other young people who could benefit from this message?

Is there a certain friend who really needs to hear the truths you've recently learned? Maybe your church youth group or Fellowship of Christian Athletes (F.C.A.) club at school would like to launch a small group study and go through the book together. Whatever the case, I encourage you to pass the message on. It is my prayer that God will use young people like you to impact our nation's youth with the truth—*the naked truth about sex and abstinence!*

For additional resources and materials, log onto *LauraGallier.com.*

A Glimpse of the Future

In closing, I'd like you to shut your eyes and imagine—wait, that won't work, will it? Okay, keep your eyes open and as you are reading, imagine…

You sit up in bed after a somewhat restless night of sleep, and already the butterflies fill your stomach. Today is one of the most important days of your entire life—your wedding day! In a matter of hours, you will stand in front of your parents, family, friends, and Almighty God and make a life-long commitment to honor and cherish the love of your life. From this moment on, you will share every day with your special soul mate until the two of you have no more days left to share.

Your mind quickly jogs back to the many memories you have already made with your fiancé—times you've laughed so hard you couldn't breathe and moments you felt such love and adoration it took your breath away. As wonderful as the memories are, excitement fills your soul to think that there are countless memories that have yet to be made!

It's time to get out of bed and get ready, but your heart is so overwhelmed with gratitude that you simply have to talk to God first. In the stillness of the moment, you begin to pray.

"Lord, I have dreamed of this day for many years, and now you have fulfilled my desire. How can I thank you for bringing me such a wonderful spouse? I am honored that you lovingly set apart such a wonderful person for me. I am both humbled and amazed at your ability to not only answer my prayers, but to pour out blessings that far exceed my expectations. May my marriage be a continual delight in your sight, Lord. May I love my precious spouse with the same devotion and passion that you have always had for me."

Now ask yourself, *was it worth the wait?*

Notes
to Me

*

Why Wait?

Why Wait?

_____

_____

_____

_____

_____

_____

_____

_____

_____

_____

_____

_____

_____

_____

_____

_____

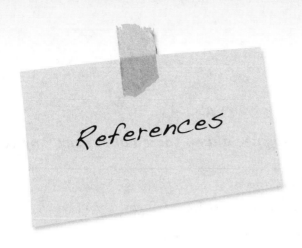

References

Chapter One

Isn't premarital abstinence for nuns and nerds?

1. Kaiser Family Foundation, "U.S. Teen Sexual Activity" doc#3040-02 (January 2005). Accessed June 22, 2009, from http://www.kff.org/youthhivstds/upload/U-S-Teen-Sexual-Activity-Fact-Sheet.pdf.

2. Ibid.

3. Kaiser Family Foundation. "U.S. Teen Sexual Activity" doc#3040-02 (January 2005). Accessed June 22, 2009, from http://www.kff.org/youthhivstds/upload/U-S-Teen-Sexual-Activity-Fact-Sheet.pdf.

4. Ibid.

5.   Ibid.

Chapter Two
What's so special and sacred about sex, anyway?

1.   Linda Lyons, "Teens' Marriage Views Reflect Changing Norms," *The Gallup Organization*, (November 18, 2003).

2.   Manda Aufochs Gillespie, "STDs and Condoms: Are You Really Safe?" Accessed July 2, 2009, from http://www.fnewsmagazine.com/2005-feb/current/pages/5.shtml.

3.   Maggie Fox, "Sex Map Shows Chain of Almost 300 High School Lovers," *Reuters*, January 24, 2005.

4.   Cheryl Wetzstein, "Sexually Transmitted Infection Rates Soar Among Youth," *The Washington Times*, March 1, 2004.

5.   Robert Rector, Kirk Johnson, and Lauren Noyes, "Sexually Active Teenagers Are More Likely to Be Depressed and to Attempt Suicide," *The Heritage Foundation* (June 3, 2003).

6.   Ibid.

Chapter Three
Why is premarital sex sometimes referred to as a sin?

1. Kathleen Stassen Berger, *The Developing Person Through the Lifespan,* 7th ed. (Bronx, New York: Worth Publishers, 2008).

2. Joyce Howard Price, "Teens Want to Wait for Sex," *The Washington Times*, December 2003.

3. Manda Aufochs Gillespie, "STDs and Condoms," Accessed July 2, 2009, from http://www.fnewsmagazine. com/2005-feb/current/pages/5.shtml.

4. Robert Rector, Kirk Johnson, and Lauren Noyes. "Sexually Active Teenagers Are More Likely to Be Depressed and to Attempt Suicide," *The Heritage Foundation* (June 3, 2003).

5. National Survey of Family Growth, "Science Says: Teens' Attitudes Toward Sexual Activity," *Science Says,* No. 14 (May 2005). http://www.thenationalcampaign.org/ resources/pdf/SS/SS14_Sex.pdf.

6. Bridget E. Maher, "Abstinence Until Marriage: The Best Message for Teens," *Family Research Council* (September 7, 2004).

7. Sue Johanson, "Talk Sex," Accessed July 2, 2009, from http://www.talksexwithsue.com/condoms.html.

Chapter Four
What's the big deal to about losing your virginity?

1. Lauren F. Winner, "Sex in the Body of Christ," *Christianity Today*, *49*, 5 (May 2005). http://www .christianitytoday.com/ct/2005/may/34.28.html.

2. M. J. Rosenberg and M. S. Waugh, "Latex Condom Breakage and Slippage in a Controlled Clinical Trial," *Contraception,* 56 (1997): 17–21.

3. Kathleen Stassen Berger, *The Developing Person Through the Lifespan*, 7th ed. (Bronx, New York: Worth Publishers, 2008). Accessed July 2, 2009, from http://www .puremorality.org/NCPCFstats.htm.

4. Elizabeth Eden, M.D., "A Guide to Pregnancy Complications," http://health.howstuffworks.com/a-guide -to-pregnancy-complications-ga2.htm.

Chapter Five
How far is going too far?

1. Sharon Jayson, "Technical Virginity Becomes Part of Teens' Equation," *USA Today*, October 19, 2005.

2. Ed Wheat M.D., and Gayle Wheat, *Intended for Pleasure: Sex Technique and Sexual Fulfillment in Christian Marriage* (Grand Rapids, MI: Fleming H. Revell, 1976), 74.

3. Caroline Stanley, "Oral Sex: A Dangerous Teen Trend," *Oral Cancer News* (March 29, 2005). http://oralcancernews.org/wp/2005/03/oral-sex-a-dangerous-teen-trend/.

4. Koss, Woodruff (1990). Koss Study. Retrieved August 15, 2000, from the World Wide Web: http://www.uga.edu/~safe-campus.

5. Sharon Jayson, "Survey: Many Teenagers Have Oral Sex," *USA Today* (September 9, 2005).

6. The National Campaign to Prevent Teen Pregnancy, "Parents and Teen Pregnancy: What Surveys Show," September 2003. Accessed October 23, 2008, from www.thenationalcampaign.org/national-data/pdf/Parentspollingfactoids2004.pdf.

Chapter Six
I could use some dating advice; got any?

1. *Sex in the Body of Christ*, Lauren F. Winner, *Christianity Today* (May 2005).

2. "Teens and Sex: Stop Worrying, Start Talking," *Better Homes and Gardens* (September 8, 2007). Accessed October 22, 2008, from www.bhg.com/health-family/parenting-skills.

3. Shannon Ethridge, "Mamas, Don't Let Your Babies Grow Up to Be Sexually Ignorant," *Enrichment Journal* (2005).

4. Kathleen Stassen Berger, *The Developing Person Through the Lifespan*, 7th ed. (Bronx, New York: Worth Publishers, 2008).

5. Ibid.

6. The Henry J. Kaiser Foundation "U.S. Teen Sexual Activity," California: 2005, 1-2. 15 Oct. 2007 www.kff.org.

7. Kathleen Stassen Berger, *The Developing Person Through the Lifespan*: 7th ed. (Bronx, New York: Worth Publishers, 2008).

8. Ibid.

9. Ibid.

10. "Nearly 3 in 10 Young Teens Sexually Active," *NBC News, People* magazine poll (January 19, 2005).

Chapter Seven

What are some common objections and rebuttals concerning abstinence?

1. Kathleen Stassen Berger, *The Developing Person Through the Lifespan*, 7th ed. (Bronx, New York: Worth Publishers, 2008).

2. The Kaiser Family Foundation, *Virginity and the First Time* (October 2003).

3. Joyce Howard Price, "Teens Want to Wait for Sex," *The Washington Times* (December 2003).

4. U.S. Department of Commerce, U.S. Census Bureau, *America's Families and Living Arrangements: 2003* (November 2004).

5. National Center for Health Statistics (December 2004), www.cdc.gov/nchs.

6. A. Zenit, "Cohabitation: A Recipe for Martial Ruin," *Daily Dispatch,* October 1, 2005.

7. "Divorce May Be the Cost of Living Together First," *New York Times*, January 30, 2008.

8. Zenit.

9. Ibid.

10. Ibid.

11. Ibid.

12. Ibid.

13. Ibid.

14. Ibid.

15. Ibid.

Chapter Eight

How does my home life and environment affect my sexual appetite?

1. Kathleen Stassen Berger, *The Developing Person Through the Lifespan*, 7th ed. (Bronx, New York: Worth Publishers, 2008).

2. Diane E. Papalia, Sally Wendkos Olds, and Ruth Duskin Feldman, *A Child's Developing Word, Infancy Through Adolescence*, 11th ed. (New York: McGraw-Hill Higher Education, 2008).

3. John Eldredge, *Wild at Heart, Discovering the Secret of a Man's Soul* (Nashville, TN: Thomas Nelson Inc., 2001), and Staci Eldredge, *Captivating: Unveiling the Mystery of a Woman's Soul* (Nashville: Thomas Nelson Inc., 2005).

4. Berger.

5. Bill Albert, *With One Voice: America's Adults and Teens Sound Off About Teen Pregnancy* (Washington DC: National Campaign to Prevent Teen Pregnancy, 2004), 6, www.thenationalcampaign.org/national-data/.

6. Berger.

7. http://www.puremorality.org/NCPCFstats.htm.

8. Ibid.

9. Ibid.

10. Papalia, Olds, and Feldman.

Chapter Nine
How do I find a mate who's right for me?

1. Kathleen Stassen Berger, *The Developing Person Through the Lifespan*, 7th ed. (Bronx, New York: Worth Publishers, 2008).

2. Diane E. Papalia, Sally Wendkos Olds, and Ruth Duskin Feldman, *A Child's Developing Word: Infancy Through Adolescence*, 11th ed. (New York: McGraw-Hill Higher Education, 2008).

3. Ibid.

4. Ibid.

5. Ibid.

6. Ibid.

7. Peter Lord, *Hearing God* (Grand Rapids, MI: Baker Book House, 1988).

8. Papalia, Olds, and Feldman.

Chapter Ten
What if I've already had sex?

1. Kathleen Stassen Berger, *The Developing Person Through the Lifespan*, 7th ed. (Bronx, New York: Worth Publishers, 2008).

2. "Nearly 3 in 10 Young Teens Sexually Active," *NBC News*, *People* magazine poll (January 19, 2005).

3. Berger.

Chapter Eleven
How in the world do I resist having sex until I'm married?

1.   Diane E. Papalia, Sally Wendkos Olds, and Ruth Duskin Feldman, *A Child's Developing Word: Infancy Through Adolescence*, 11th ed. (New York: McGraw-Hill Higher Education, 2008).

2.   Ibid.

About the
Author

*M*otivated by a passion for the preservation of family values, Laura B. Gallier has spent the last decade as a youth minister and advisor to teens and parents. Laura is known for her unique ability to effectively address today's most controversial social issues in a down-to-earth, biblical way. She and her husband, Patrick, live in Cypress, Texas, and maintain an adventurous home life that consists of three children, two hermit crabs, a dog, and one highly temperamental fish!

To learn more about how you can launch a "Why Wait?" inspiring abstinence campaign in your church, school, or community, log onto **LauraGallier.com**.